Avoiding the Cracks

A personal odyssey
and a story of survival
1939 to 1949

Rudy Horowitz

1

ISBN-13: 978-1495497261

Cover design by Rudy Horowitz.

2nd Edition December 2016

3rd Edition March 2018

For Diana and David

TABLE OF CONTENTS

PREFACE

Most of the milestone events in my early life happened at decade intervals beginning in 1929, the year I was born, in Sosnowiec Poland. It was the year the stock market

Me at 6 months with Dad, Mom and Oskar in the country. Summer 1929

crashed in America, triggering a ten-year long worldwide economic depression. In 1939 when I was ten, the Second World War broke out after Hitler invaded Poland. Ten years later, in 1949, I arrived with my brother, Oscar, in the United States.

7

My story is a collection of "letters forward" to my grand-children, Oscar, and Emma who may not have me around as they grow to adulthood. It will introduce them to the world of my childhood and youth. It will also acquaint them with some of my family who perished during the war and until this writing were a nameless collection of discarded photographs in an old shoebox.

The events in my narrative are all true as far as my memory serves me. In some instances I use invented names for persons who may be peripheral to my narrative, or whose names I no longer remember. The same may be true with respect to exact dates of events unique to my memoir.

In other instances where the events had a general, historical significance I availed myself of an excellent monograph written in Polish by Mgr. Natan Elias Sternfinkel entitled "Zagłada Zydów Sosnowca" (The Annihilation of Sosnowiec Jews), It offers detail of day by day transgressions and atrocities perpetrated by the Nazis on the Jewish in habitants of my home town.

The title of my narrative comes from a ritual I engaged in while in the Srodula Ghetto, at the height of the deportation of Jews to Auschwitz in 1942-1943. Whenever I ran to or from home – I never walked at that age -- I tried to avoid the cracks in the pavement telling myself that no harm would come to us if I don't step on them, and that this would help us survive the war.

Guilford, summer, 2013

PROLOGUE

My father, Paul Peilet Horowitz was born on April 17, 1897 in Drohobycz, Poland, which at the time of his birth was part of the Austria-Hungarian Empire. My paternal grandfather's, Osias Fastman, and my grandmother's, (her last name was Horowitz), ritual wedding was not recognized by the authorities, hence their offspring had to take on their mother's name. My grandfather came to America in 1900 to seek his fortune and after going back home for a brief period, returned to the U.S. in 1906 where he stayed until he died in the Spanish flu pandemic in 1918. My father's two brothers, Leon, and Harry immigrated to America in the early 1920's.

Father in WW I

Meanwhile, Father who excelled in his studies graduated from the Polish gymnasium (high school) and joined the Legions of Marshal Pilsudski who took up arms for Polish independence during the First World War. He spent time in the Polish fledgling air corps, flying in rickety bi-planes as an ob-

10

server. After the, war following demobilization, he gained admission to the medical school at the University of Lwow, from which he graduated with a Medical Degree in May 1926. His graduation was to be followed by a year of residency in his chosen field of ophthalmology, in Vienna, Austria.

That summer, while vacationing at a mountain resort in

Poland, he was summoned to the bedside of a patient suffering from a bad cold and running a fever. My mother, Pola Lancman, was his patient. Leaving for Vienna after his vacation, he began a busy correspondence with her which ultimately became a whirlwind long distance courtship, and which culminated in their wedding on

Mom and Dad, Vienna 1927

January 2nd 1927. They spent their honeymoon in Vienna and stayed on for nearly a year. Mother enjoyed living in Vienna but she missed her parents and siblings terribly. Moreover, expecting the arrival of my brother Oskar in January, they returned to Sosnowiec, Mother's birthplace. They decided to

Oskar and I in 1931

11

settle there renting a large apartment on the ground floor of a newly completed five story building two doors down from my grandparents' home.

Grandfather, Grandmother and uncle Josef in Krynica Spa 1936

My grandfather, Lew Lancman was a prosperous merchant. He owned a large man's haberdashery store and a four-story apartment building. Together with my grandmother Brenda Rachel Lancman they traveled a great deal spending a couple of months a year in various spas and resorts. Mother had a sister, Regina, and three brothers, Josef, Henry and Mietek. She had two half-brothers and a half-sister from grandfather's first marriage. Anshel was a salesman who lavished us with halvah and armies of tin soldiers on his frequent visits. David whom we never met lived in London. Karola lived in Lodz with her three children but seldom came to see us.

12

Father had an affinity for Vienna and did not give up on settling there eventually. Our given names, Oskar and Rudolf, are no doubt a testament to his wish to live in Vienna, as they were more common in Austria than in Poland. He loved the opera, concerts, art galleries and the cultural life of that cosmopolitan city, few of which were available in Sosnowiec. Every year he would spend a month at the Vienna clinic honing his medical skills and soaking up the culture. He continued this until 1938, the year of the Anschluss, when Hitler marched into Austria and the persecution of Jews began.

Uncle Henry, Mom and Dad skiing in Zakopane, 1937

Mother, an avid skier, spent every February skiing in Zakopane, a Polish ski resort, leaving us in the care of Nanny, and Father. In the spring and autumn Mother played tennis in a park next to my elementary school.

Sometimes she brought me along to pick up the balls for her.

July and August of every summer we would spend with mother in the country. Frequently she rented primitive accommodations in a farmer's house, with no electricity or running water and the ubiquitous out-house. Some of my fondest memories go back to those summers. The farmer's children whom we be-friended could run faster jump higher, throw rocks farther that either of us could ever hope to. Most impres-sive was their ability to walk and run barefoot on freshly mowed fields of grain, which to us seemed worse than walking on nails.

Me, Uncle Henry and Oskar on vacation in Węgierska Górka, summer 1936

Alternatively we would spend summers at elegant villas with all the comforts of a fine hotel.

Father was a strict disciplinarian. Our playtime was closely supervised and our friends were properly screened. We were not allowed to play out in the street with other kids for fear we might pick up bad language and bad habits.

Although there was a private, secular, Jewish school in Sosnowiec, Father and Mother enrolled us in a public school in the firm belief that religion had nothing to do with education. The result was that Oskar and I were the only Jewish boys in our respective classes. There was a crucifix hanging above the teacher's desk in every class-room and each morning began with the Lord's Prayer. I had to stand silently with my arms at my sides as the other children crossed themselves and recited the pray-er. This attracted the attention of some classroom bullies who showered me with anti-Semitic slurs and knocked my hat off whenever I walked past the big church on my way home. The other boys and girls made the sign of the cross or tipped their hats which I did not do.

In order to avoid passing the church, I frequently did something Father did not approve of. I took an alternate route home, through the commercial district past Grand-pa's store, where Grandma greeted me with very wet kisses and took me to the candy store next door where I got my favorite candy box containing candy and a hid-den treasure of foreign postage stamps for my stamp collection.

To compensate for the public school, Father and Mother engaged Mr. Fishel, a private tutor to teach us modern Hebrew. He came to our home twice weekly, after school, and by the time I was in fourth grade I was quite proficient in the language.

Despite the worldwide depression we were quite well off during the years leading up to the World War II. Recognizing this fact Mother always gave me two sandwiches for my school lunch, so that I could offer one to a boy who did not have any lunch.

My childhood and school years leading up to World War II were full of happy memories. All that changed in 1939.

June 29th 1939

Dear Oscar and Emma,

I am 10 years old now. Somehow I feel more grown up. My age is made up of two digits, just like the grown-ups. School is over and I just finished 4th grade.

School was quite different this year than in years past. Hitler is beating the drums of war and threatening to invade Poland. At the pupils assemble daily at noon in the school hallways to sing patriotic songs. The school bulletin board is plastered with pictures of marching soldiers and of squadrons of Polish bombers and fighter planes.

At home, Father sits on a stool in front of the radio, his elbows on his knees, face cradled in his hands, eyes shut, listening intently to the barking sounds of Hitler delivering yet another hate filled speech. Frequently, after listening to one of the speeches, Father turns to Mother suggesting that we all pack up and go to the New York World's Fair. Of course, she will not have any of that. She will not leave her family.

Uncle Henry and Jozef practice short order drill on their visits to our home, in anticipation of being drafted into the army. It is amusing to see grown men barking orders, and stomping around the living room like little kids playing soldier.

Oskar, Mother and I in 1939

Despite these disturbing signals, Oskar and I are very excited as this is the first time we are going on vacation without Mother. We will spend the month of July in a boy-scout camp run by a Zionist organization. It is supposed to be quite primitive and harsh. We are looking forward to camping and roughing it. We will spend the month of August in a luxurious children's camp in Ustron, to recover from the hardships of the previous month.

I am signing off for now, with love and kisses,

Your loving future Papa

September 15th, 1939

Dear Oscar and Emma,

I am writing this letter from Żolynia in south central Poland. Sorry I did not write to you sooner, but a lot of bad
things happened since my last letter. Worst of all, Hitler
invaded on September 1st, and by now occupied most of
Poland.

When I last wrote, we were just about to leave for camp.
The Boy Scout camp, which is run by the Zionist organization Hanoar Hatzioni, turned out to be just what I expected. We did a lot of camping, singing hiking and
swimming. Unfortunately we did not meet anyone we
knew, there, so it did not turn out to be as enjoyable as I
expected. Conversely, the camp in Ustron was a lot more
fun. We knew a bunch of boys and girls from our
hometown. The best thing that happened to me was that
Richard Dugot a boy from my home town taught me to
ride on his two-wheeler

Although we were supposed to stay there till the end of
August, Mother arrived on August 24th to take us home.

Father's reserve unit was called up and he was to report to the field hospital in Cracow. We were to join him there as soon as we returned from camp.

We arrived in Cracow on the last day of August and checked into a hotel room near the main Market Square. Next day, on September 1st the German Army invaded Poland. Since Cracow was less than 100 miles from the German border, Father thought it would be unsafe for us to stay there and after consulting the map he picked the city of Lublin in central Poland as a much safer place for the time being. That same afternoon he went to the train station and got us tickets for the Lublin express scheduled to leave at noon on September 3rd.

An atmosphere of gloom had taken over the city of Cracow. People were visibly depressed walking around as if in a trance. Rumors were rampant. Stories of rapid German advances and the collapse of Polish defenses were heard on every street corner. Unfortunately, most of these stories turned out to be true.

On the morning of the 3rd, as we were packing for our trip, we heard a great commotion in the street below. The news just came over the radio that England and France declared war on Germany. The atmosphere of gloom turned to instant jubilation. People were laughing, congratulating each other, and hugging and kissing strangers in the street. For sure the war would be over in a matter of days with the total collapse of the Nazi forces.

Our plans remained unchanged, as Father escorted us with our luggage to the train station to catch the train for Lublin. As we settled in our compartment, Oskar and I grabbed the two seats close to the window. I then pulled on the leather strap, which lowers the window so I could lean out, and observe the commotion and activities on the platform below us. Immediately opposite our track there was a train with a mixture of passenger cars and freight cars. The passenger cars were filled with officers and the freight cars with enlisted men. The soldiers were all laughing and singing and joking about giving it to the Germans.

Suddenly, out of nowhere I felt a tremendous blast of air accompanied by an ear-shattering explosion. It knocked me off my feet and I landed in Mother's lap. I then realized that the drone of plane engines preceded the explosion. Now there were explosions all around us. The Nazi dive-bombers were after the troop train, and we found ourselves in the middle of the air raid.

Someone yelled "Everyone get off the train"

Mother grabbed us by the hand and rushed for the exit. Most of the other compartments as well as the corridor were filled with wounded women and children bleeding

21

profusely. The blasts of the explosions blew out all the windows of the compartments in which the windows remained shut, and the shards of glass became deadly projectiles, killing and wounding any one in their paths. Running and stepping over the casualties and through pools of blood we got off the train and rushed down the stairs to the underground passage between the train platforms. The space was jammed with humanity, mainly women with children, some covered with blood, screaming and praying. The bombs kept raining down for seemingly an interminable amount of time, though it probably was no more than 15 minutes. With each explosion, Mother grabbed our heads pulling us toward her to shield us beneath her body.

After the bombs stopped falling, the drone of the planes receded into the distance, and the all-clear siren sounded, we emerged from our underground shelter and headed back for the hotel. The devastation at the station was complete. Overturned railway cars some in pieces, twisted rails were everywhere. Throngs of men and women with Red Cross armbands were tending to the wounded and the dead carrying them on stretchers to waiting ambulances and trucks. At the hotel we went straight to our room, which was still registered in Father's name.

About an hour later Father appeared at the door, his face ashen. He put his arms around us and told us that he knew we survived the bombing and were alive. As it happened, all the casualties from the train were sent to his hospital, so after going through the wards to check the wounded, and not seeing us there, he went to the basement morgue to look for us among the dead. Only then did he come back to the hotel.

Offering the hotel porter a very generous tip, Father asked him to go back to our train to retrieve our luggage. To my amazement he did so successfully and brought everything back without a single piece missing.

Since going on by train was now out of the question, Mother and Father decided we would spend the rest of the day recovering from the trauma, and think about what to do next on the following day.

When I woke up the next morning Father had already left for the hospital. He returned just as we were finishing breakfast. He appeared very rushed and agitated. After stopping a random car in the street and questioning the driver for a couple of minutes he determined that the driver was heading east, away from the advancing Germans. Since the driver was all alone he consented to take the three of us along.

It took us only a few minutes to load our bags in the trunk, and after hugging and kissing Father goodbye, we were off. The car was an Autounion convertible, with its familiar four rings insignia. After the traumatic experience of the previous day, Oskar and I were happy and excited about this new experience, never having ridden in a convertible with a top down before.

We drove through the towns of Tarnów, Rzeszów, Łancut, all along dodging multitudes of refugees heading east, both on foot and in horse drawn hay wagons. Because of these crowds and the poor road conditions it took us nearly six hours to drive a distance of some 120 miles.

That is when we arrived in the village of Żołynia, which could be characterized more accurately as a shtetl straight out of a Shalom Aleichem story. In addition to the local farmers and peasants, it had a large community of bearded, orthodox Jews clad in black caftans. Our

24

driver decided that this would be our destination, unloading our luggage and bidding us goodbye. We met some of the locals and after Mother introduced herself, we were invited to the home of one of the village elders. Mr. Szpilman, a prosperous local merchant with a large family welcomed us with open arms and asked us to stay through the holidays. Rosh Hashanah, the Jewish New Year, was only a few days away.

The accommodations were very primitive complete with outhouse and no running water. It reminded me of some of our summer vacations on Polish farms. Nevertheless the hospitality of our hosts made up for the relative discomfort and crowded conditions.

Three days ago the Germans marched into Żołynia. At first I wasn't sure they were Germans. I was used to seeing the Nazis in my comic books and on school bulletin boards dressed in brown shirts with giant swastikas on their armbands. These troops were wearing gray-green uniforms and the tanks and trucks had a strange looking cross painted on them. Perhaps, they are French troops coming to Poland's rescue, I speculated. My doubts were dispelled quickly, though, as they got closer. They all had a small insignia of an eagle straddling a swastika on their chests.

On the following day the Germans posted a bulletin in German and Polish directing all the Jews of Żołynia to leave the village at once and head across the San River to the east of us. This coincided with rumors that Soviet troops were occupying the eastern part of Poland, up to the San River. The elders of the village decided to ignore the directive for the time being, as the first day of the Jewish New Year fell on the following day, which was yesterday.

Not knowing Father's whereabouts and unwilling to venture east into the unknown, the only option left to us is to head back to Sosnowiec. With the help of our host Mother made arrangements with a local peasant to take us back to our hometown in his horse drawn hay wagon. The trip will take several days and the driver will be compensated accordingly. We are leaving bright and early tomorrow morning.

I will write to you again as soon as I can,

With love and devotion,

Your future Papa

December 1st 1939

Dear Oscar and Emma,

More bad things happened since I last wrote to you.

Compared to our trip by car going east, the return trip by horse drawn wagon was very slow and uncomfortable. It took us several days to get back to Sosnowiec. Our farmer-driver got help from farms along the way, where he fed and rested his horse while we spent the nights in barns sleeping on piles of hay.

Back home, we saw the immediate effects of the Nazi occupation everywhere. Grandfather told us that on September 5th, the day after the Germans entered Sosnowiec, he was arrested along with hundreds of Jewish men of all ages and kept in the cellar of the Town Hall for several days without food or water. When the Germans asked for a representative of the Jewish community to step forward, no one responded. Finally, a man named Moniek Meryn a local never-do-well with no prior standing in the community stepped forward. The Germans, after first beating him up and kicking him, designated him as the head of the Jewish community, or "Judenrat" and liaison to the Gestapo. The people were gradually released, with the oldest going home first. Grandfather's hair and beard had been cut off and when he finally came home he looked gaunt and emaciated. Some nev- er returned as they were shot for a variety of minor transgressions.

In the first week of November we were directed to vacate our apartment, leaving all our possessions, except for personal clothing. All Jews living on our street and sev- eral other streets in the more prosperous part of town met with the same fate. German families, who followed

the army into Poland, now occupy all these apartments.

We moved in with our grandpar- ents, taking over Uncle Jozef's room. The room is vacant since uncles Jozef and Henry left for the Soviet zone in the east.

Gustav and little Sara

Aunt Regina, the "black sheep" of the family, has a son, Gustav, who is Oskar's age and a daughter, Sara who is four-year-old. She is divorced and she is leaving Gustav with his father, and little Sara with my grandmother. She too, is going to the Soviet zone, abandoning her children.

28

Oskar and I, no longer lead the prewar sheltered life under the watchful eye of Father and we go about freely mixing with kids and making new friends out in the street.

A bright moment dispelled the misery of the Nazis presence, last month when a postcard arrived from Father. He is in Bucharest, Romania, where he was evacuated with his Army unit. He is anxious for us to join him there. Mother is elated to hear that he is alive and well.

Just about the same time the Germans issue several edicts, which make life even more difficult. All Jews above the age of 12 must wear a white armband with a blue Star of David on their left arm. Some young women defy this rule by wearing stylish capes. All Jewish businesses including Grandfather's store must engage a gentile trustee to take charge, and eventually turn it over into German hands. Public schools no longer accept Jewish pupils. There are sporadic shootings and hangings. Young, able-bodied men and women are snatched off the street and sent to labor camps. There is a complete blackout along with a strict curfew for all the Jews, and no one is allowed out in the street after 7 pm.

Mother tried to shield us from all of this, to no avail. To restore some sense of normalcy she engages Mr. Danziger, a young college freshman to tutor us in public school subjects. He spends two hours every morning with us, giving us enough homework to keep us busy the better part of each afternoon. She also engages Miss. Matlis to teach us English. Miss Matlis is an attractive spinster who had spent some years living in England. To my ignorant ears she sounds like an English native. Oskar and I eagerly embrace the opportunity to learn English.

Mother contacts a number of "fixers" (men who claim to have contacts and influence with the German authorities), to find a way out of Poland to Romania to join Father. She spends a lot of money to pay them off as well as their German contacts. Regrettably, all their efforts meet with failure.

Sorry I cannot end this letter on a more cheerful note.

Your loving future Papa

December 7ᵗʰ 1940

Dear Oscar and Emma,

It's over a year since my last letter. I was all set to write to you in the Summer, but I broke my right shoulder and collar bone while play-wrestling with one of the neighborhood kids At first I thought that the pain would eventually go away, so I tried to exercise my arm in the shower. The pain grew progressively worse until it became unbearable. I finally told Mother what happened and she took me to see the doctor immediately. Dr. Melodysta, an old family friend and colleague of Father's X-rayed my shoulder and determined that there were two hairline fractures in my shoulder and collarbone. We went from his office directly to the hospital where an orthopedic surgeon placed my arm against my chest and wrapped my entire torso in a wet bandage impregnated with starch. I spent the next hour in the boiler room next to the water heater waiting for it to dry. As it dried it kept shrinking making it difficult for me to take a deep breath. The lightweight cast stayed on for five weeks, which was followed by two weeks of physical therapy.

Letter writing was out of the question. My biggest worry was keeping up with my schoolwork and English lessons. I managed to do some lame scribbling with my left hand, and when things got too difficult, Oskar helped me with my homework.

Thankfully, we are making good progress with our English. Miss M. taught us the refrain from an old English folk song:

> *Do you remember the path where we met*
> *Long long ago, long long ago*
> *There you have told me you never would forget*
> *Long long ago, long long ago*

About a month after I completely recovered I had another mishap. Mother sent me on an errand to borrow a neighbor's electric iron. The neighbor's apartment was across the courtyard in the rear of our building. Though it was past curfew, it did not involve going out in the street, so it was safe for me to go there. With a moonless over- cast sky and the mandatory blackout I was literally blind crossing the courtyard. While I managed that and got the iron, on my way back I missed the gateway to the front apartment building and tripped and fell into a stair area-way leading to the basement. I landed on my forehead having no idea what happened and where I was. Feeling my way around, I found the stairs in front of me and climbed up on all fours eventually getting back to our apartment. I must have been a sight. I had a nasty deep cut above my left eyebrow, and by now my face was covered with blood. Although Mother was in shock, she wrapped towels around my forehead, and ignoring the curfew took me across the street to a nearby clinic. We were in luck. The clinic was still open and there was a dental surgeon in attendance. He cleaned and sterilized the wound and using a surgical stapler closed it with three staples. We were back home in less that an hour.

Although Mother keeps trying to shield us from the increasing terror of the German persecution of Jews, seeing and hearing what is happening around us is unavoidable. At the end of last year food rationing coupons were introduced, with individual rations of 7 ounces of bread daily and a weekly ration of 3.5 ounces each of margarine, sugar and jam. Initially, it was possible to purchase additional foodstuffs on the black market from the Polish side of the town, but as shortages are growing in and out of the ghettos this is becoming increasingly more difficult. Bread and potatoes are scarce and expensive. Turnips, the kind normally fed to cattle, are the only vegetable available in profusion. They are prepared in many different forms, but I've grown to dislike them intensely, and I gag at the mere sight and smell of them.

Mrs. Jaworska is the one bright spot in our meager, monotonous diet. She and her husband own a dairy farm about an hour's train ride from Sosnowiec. Before the war she made the trip every Friday bringing fresh cream, cottage cheese and butter from her farm to us and to Grandmother. Somehow, she still manages to do it once a month or so, despite the fact that the Germans confiscate most of the farm output for themselves.

At the beginning of the year the Germans exacted a heavy head-tax from every Jew in Sosnowiec. Those unable to pay were subject to immediate deportation. The Jewish Committee under the direction of Moniek Meryn was assigned the task of collecting the money and delivering it to the Germans.

Later this spring another directive demanded the surrender of all precious metals, in all forms: gold rings, bracelets and other jewelry, silver cutlery, candelabras, goblets, platters and so on. Severe penalties would befall any who failed to comply with this order. My grandpar- ents had no intention of giving up their precious posses- sions to the Nazis. While small items of jewelry were easy to conceal within their home, the silver candela- bras, goblets and platters and such were much too large to keep around. Grandfather got hold of two very large breadboxes and carefully packed the silverware in them, along with stacks of Polish banknotes in large denominations. He enlisted my help in burying this "treasure". Since his store was not yet fully taken over by the Germans, he still had access to it and kept a spare set of keys at home. On a Sunday evening he took one of the heavy boxes and a small fireplace shovel and, with me tagging along, went to the store. Since the basement floor was unpaved it was not too difficult to dig a hole in the dirt and bury the box in it. We spread the excess dirt throughout the basement and covered it with excess boxes and packing material, which were stored there.

In the courtyard of grandfather's apartment house there were individual wooden storage lockers for each tenant. Grandfather had two such lockers for his own use. Here, too, the floor of the lockers was unpaved and we buried the second box in one of the lockers. After the job was done, Grandfather said to me that if he does not survive the war, I would be there to retrieve his "treasure".

Like all homes in the ghetto, Grandparents' apartment is getting more crowded. Two days ago Mr. and Mrs. Wachtel, an elderly couple arrived from Oswiecim (Auschwitz) and moved in with us. They along with the entire Jewish population of Oswiecim were transplanted to Sosnowiec and neighboring towns. No doubt, the Germans are planning something and when they plan it cannot be good.

Another bit of bad news arrived this week in a postcard from Archangelsk in northern Russia. Aunt Regina died of typhus, leaving little Sara in grandma's care. Gustav stays with his father and visits infrequently. Though he is very street smart and has a good command of German he is extremely foolhardy. Last time he showed up wearing a Hitlerjugend[1] jacket and hat with the swastika in-signia on it. I am very fond of him but I fear for his safety.

Until my next letter, I'll try to avoid wrestling in fun and.falling into basements.

Your loving future Papa

---

[1] the Nazi version of Boy Scouts

September 10th, 1941

Dear Oscar and Emma,

Recent events, most of them unpleasant, prevented me from writing sooner. Never mind that referring to what the Nazis are doing to us, as unpleasantness is the height of understatement.

I will bring you up to date presently, but first I want to share the latest indigni- ty, which befell us this week. Starting last Mon- day all Jews from the age of six must wear a yellow Star of David with the word Jude (Jew) on their left breast. The stars are printed on cheap yellow muslin sheets in an interlocking pattern and are distributed by the Judenrat office. After cutting them apart with scis-sors, each must be sewn on securely to garments in-tended for outdoor wear.

Thus Oskar and I who were hitherto exempt from wear-ing the white armband with the Star of David will now carry with us this badge wherever we go. The word "Jude" is spelled in a mock Hebrew font. Is this the Nazis sense of humor? Additionally, all males must add the middle name, Israel, to their ID card; all women must add the middle name, Sara. I am now Rudolf Israel Horowitz.

Mother, along with many other unfortunates is trying to defy and outsmart the Germans in whatever small way is possible. In response to the directive that all fur coats have to be turned in, she had her fur turned inside out and altered so that it looks like an ordinary winter coat with the fur concealed in the lining. When they demanded that all ski boots be turned in for the use of the Wehrmacht she had the ski boots altered by a shoemaker so that the distinguishing square toe which fits into a bear-trap binding was rounded on a shoe last,. Now Oskar and I, each have a pair of hiking boots.

Early in the spring the Central Jewish Committee assisted the Germans in organizing workshops of various trades in the ghetto. The Committee sent out appeals to tradesman and craftsmen to join these workshops and thus be safe from deportation. The first shop organized by a German entrepreneur from Berlin, Hans Held, eager to profit from cheap labor employs tailors who turn out military uniforms and various other articles of clothing. It was followed by Schwedler's shop, which manufactures leather goods, principally rucksacks for the military.

By this time Oskar and I unencumbered by the slow pro-gress in a conventional public school completed three years of instruction with our tutor, and we were far ahead of other kids our age. Mother dismissed the tutor, though we are continuing with our English lessons.

Early in June Mrs. Jaworska, our dairy farm lady offered to take Oskar and myself to her farm for a couple of weeks to fatten us up with decent peasant fare and let us breathe some fresh country air. Though it was risky, Mother consented and off we went to the farm. Our stay there brought back memories of the carefree prewar summers we spent on the farm. Unfortunately we had to return home after a week. The Germans had just invaded the Soviet Union, and all the military traffic going through the village on the way East made Mrs. Jaworska very nervous, so she brought us back to Sosnowiec.

Like some other children over the age of twelve we went to work in the shops. Oskar was hired by the Schwedler leather shop and learned how to mend leather back-packs.

I had the good fortune to get work in an art shop, which was owned by a German woman related to Schwedler. It is a small enterprise employing about 50 people. I am the only child working there. The shop turns out decorative designs, mainly flowers, on ceramic tiles, which are sold as wall hangings. My job is to fill in flower petals on the tile designs with a small paint brush, matching the colors of an approved sample. I work with 20 or 25 tiles in front of me all inked with the outlines of the flowers, mixing a color for each petal and filling them in one at a time on all the tiles. When one petal is complete, I mix the paint for the next petal, and so on. Painting the shadings and highlights follows. Art was my hobby from an early age, and I enjoy this work regarding it more as play. For my efforts I am paid the meager sum of 14 Marks per month.

Another popular product is aphorisms carefully lettered in Gothic font on varnished wooden plaques. Though I can't do this calligraphy myself, I memorized one such aphorism in particular because of its raunchy content:

Und wieder ist ein Tag vollbracht
Und wieder ist nur Mist gemacht
Und nun lebt wohl ihr Sorgen
Leck mich am Arsch bis Morgen
Und Morgen mit dem selben Fleisse
Geht's wieder an die selbe Scheisse

Translated freely into English by yours truly:
So another day ends with a snap
And all we have made is more crap

So lay down your sorrow
Kiss my ass until tomorrow
And tomorrow with the same grit
Right back into the same shit

Though a teenager trapped by fate and the Nazis in the ghetto, I am not immune from snickering at dirty language.

It is now becoming increasingly clear why the Wachtels along with all other Jews from Oswiecim were moved to Sosnowiec and surrounding communities. Rumors abound about a huge concentration camp, which is taking shape in Oswiecim (Auschwitz) for the principal purpose of exterminating the Jews. The camp is purported to be complete with gas chambers and crematoria intended to accomplish that goal. While not all rumors turn out to be true, the ones which bring bad news generally are.

There is now even more reason to be employed in the shops that are essential to the German war effort. Though no one wishes to help the Germans, if this is the only way to save oneself, it must be done.

On this sad note I send you my love,

Your devoted future Papa

June 12th 1942

Dear Oscar and Emma,

Last February, while at work in the art shop I experienced a sharp pain in my right lung, whenever I took a deep breath. I went home feeling weak and feverish. After taking my temperature and determining that I was running a high fever, Mother sent Oskar to fetch Dr. Rzendowski a friend of the family and a colleague of Father's. The Doctor diagnosed my problem as pleurisy, explaining that it is the inflammation of the pleura which is the sack hold- ing the lung. The inflammation causes the pleura to fill with fluid and this is what causes the pain. Since there were no medicines available to deal with my condition, he prescribed bed rest and restricted fluid intake.

I stayed in bed for the next three weeks, suffering from chest pain and unbearable thirst. Dr. Rzendowski came to see me every other day, performing a percussion examination of my right lung to determine the level of the fluid. At the beginning of the third week the fluid started to recede, the fever was gone and I was out of bed on the following weekend. Though I am extremely weak and there is still pain when I breathe, I feel a lot better.

I lost my job at the art shop because of my long absence which upset me terribly. As consolation I got a position at the Schwedler leather shop, where Oskar is working.

By now he is quite experienced and he helps me in mastering hand stitching of leather using a pushpin and twin needles.

Meanwhile, more and more able-bodied men and women not employed in the shops are being snatched off the streets and shipped to labor camps in Germany. The Jewish ghetto militia and executive arm of Meryn's committee assist the Germans in this endeavor. The militiamen are distinguished from other civilians by a white policeman's cap with a blue Star of David insignia. Many of them wear expensive black leather riding boots, the common footwear of German officers and the Gestapo. Though most militiamen are decent individuals, some try to ingratiate themselves with their Nazi masters, by barking orders in German and mistreating the unfortunates they apprehend.

Now that the giant death camp in Auschwitz is no longer a rumor, the Germans are intent on filling it with Jews. To that end they issued an order to The Jewish Committee in May to deliver 5000 souls to the school building at Deblinska Street by the 10th of that month for the purpose of "relocation". Each person was limited to baggage not exceeding 10 kilograms. The Committee and the militia were unsuccessful in meeting that quota, and only a fraction of that number was delivered to the Germans. The Germans took over. They moved in at night with trucks, searchlights, barking dogs, police and Gestapo armed with machine guns, and surrounded several buildings in the ghetto. One of the buildings was Targowa St No. 2. We live in the adjacent building at No. 4.

I have never been so scared in my life. The sound of jack boots on the pavement, the barking of orders in German, the drone of the truck engines, slamming of doors, cries of women and children make me so fearful that I get a terrible case of loose bowels on an empty stomach. I expect that any instant our door will be broken down and we will be sent to our doom.

Gradually, over the next two hours, the horror subsides. It looks like we are left to live another day.

On that sad note I will sign off for now,

Your loving future Papa

October 26th, 1942

My Dear Oscar and Emma,

Just when you think things cannot get any worse, they do.

At the beginning of August the Jewish Committee appealed to the public to comply with the Gestapo order to present themselves at a giant Union soccer field on the 12th of the month for the purpose of review and validating of documents. All the buildings in the ghetto were plastered with placards appealing for compliance with the order on said date.

Everyone was wary of such orders, knowing that they inevitably lead to deportation to Auschwitz. In order to gain confidence of the Jews, the Germans conducted a similar review of identity documents in three, small, neighboring ghettos. In these localities the activity was limited to stamping of papers and all the Jews returned to their homes.

On that day we were allowed to leave the ghetto and walk freely on all the streets of Sosnowiec, previously off limits to Jews since September 1939. Since early morning of that Wednesday, the streets of Sosnowiec were filled with masses of Jews hurrying toward the Union sports stadium. Among them were men, young and old, women and children, even the sick from the hospital. Only the most gravely ill and infirm were allowed to remain in hospital upon presentation of proof of their condition to the Nazis. My grandfather was one of those seriously ill individuals and had been in the hospital for a couple of weeks. The only other ones who remained and hid were Jews who had no documents. My grandmother and little cousin Sara were among the hidden ones.

The Jewish population numbering about 26,000 arrived at the stadium, where the Gestapo and the SS armed with machine guns surrounded us. Small tables were placed in a row according to the alphabet and everyone had to register his name at the appropriate table. After the registration the Gestapo crowded everyone at one end side of the stadium, leaving the other side vacant.

It was a very hot day, and the congestion was terrible. There was a feeling of imminent danger and we were all panic-stricken.

All families were ordered to appear before a commission who would make a life or death decision for all assembled. The Commission was made up of Gestapo representatives and members of the Judenrat. Every Jew was evaluated and assigned to one of four groups, 1, 2,3, and 4. The groups were directed to different locations in the vacant part of the stadium.

Families, with all members employed and without children or elderly, were assigned number 1, their documents were stamped and they were released.

Young people, who were not employed by the shops, were assigned number 2, to be sent to a Labor Camp.

Families who had some members employed and had children were assigned number 3 and were subject to further review.

Women with children, the unemployed, and the elderly were placed in group 4. This group was destined for deportation. My mother, my brother and I were placed in that group.

Night fell and rain began to fall. We were all soaked through and hungry and little children wailed and cried. People were exhausted and couldn't stand up, sitting down and lying down on the rain-soaked ground.

During the night some people in our group, attempted to save themselves by sneaking over to group 3, but the Gestapo noticed it and started shooting. The tumult and confusion led the Gestapo to combine the two groups into one, of some 10,000 people all designated for deportation. We stayed there until the evening of the next day when we were escorted under blazing search lights in groups of a few thousand each by heavily armed Gestapo, and crowded into four buildings vacated for that purpose. My grandparents' apartment where we lived was in one of those buildings

We found ourselves crowded into our own apartment with a few hundred other people. Gestapo, German Po- lice and Jewish Militia surrounded the buildings.

We knew we were condemned to death and merely waited for transport. Overcrowding was unbearable. People were suffocating from lack of air. Some leaped to their death from fifth and sixth story windows. Some people went insane. Most were completely resigned, but some tried to save their lives. In one instance I saw a man perched on the sill of an open fifth story window. Just as he was ready to jump a German guard in the court yard aimed his rifle at him and started screaming at him. The man stepped back and disappeared. I wonder what went through his mind.

One group broke through a wall in a basement of an adjoining building and escaped. Some others escaped over roofs of adjacent structures. Some hid in empty carts, which were used to deliver bread to the victims.

My mother left disguised as a nurse, with the brave assistance of Dr. Rzendowski wearing his ubiquitous white coat and stethoscope around his neck. Just about the same time I started looking for Oskar to tell him that Mother was saved. I was astonished to find him in a rear ground floor apartment perched on a pile of bedding calmly reading a book. A few hours after Mother's escape my brother and I were led out by Dr. Rzendowski who gave two bottles of whiskey to an already drunk German guard, telling him that our mother was a nurse working for him.

During the next three days approximately 8,000 exhausted old people, women and children, some of them sick or dying were packed into cattle cars and deported to Auschwitz and their death.

A week later my grandfather who was sick in the hospital died of a heart attack upon hearing a false report that Mother, Oskar and I were in that transport. It was odd to think of his death as a bittersweet event. Dying a natural death of old age was something to be thankful for. Grandma, Mother, Oskar and I were the only ones attending his primitive funeral and burial. We followed a man behind a two-wheeled pushcart holding the body wrapped in a white shroud to the cemetery. There, Grandfather was buried unceremoniously in an unmarked grave.

Oskar and I are still working at the Schwedler shop. There are a lot fewer people there now. This is also true of the rest of the ghetto. The Wachtels are gone. They were deported in August. It is sad and ironical that they went back to their hometown, Oswiecim, Auschwitz to meet their end at the hand of the Nazi assassins.

At the beginning of this month the Germans announced that they will be relocating the ghetto to the suburb of Srodula and consolidating it with ghettos of adjacent communities. Srodula is a low-income Polish working class neighborhood, occupied mainly by laborers, coal miners and their families. The Judenrat is supposed to pay for the relocation of the Poles to homes previously occupied by the Jews in Sosnowiec.

Although we get frequent letters from Father in Bucharest, Mother cannot communicate our ordeals directly, as all the mail is censored by the German military. She uses code words to describe what is happening to us hoping that he will understand our misfortunes.

Mother tries to cheer us up and distract us from this brutal reality, but it is impossible to shield us anymore. We are now full participants in everything that is happening daily around us. On that sad note, I'll end this letter, hoping to write to you again soon.

Your loving future Papa.

April 15th 1943

My Dear Oscar and Emma,

We have moved to Srodula at the beginning of the year and are living in a tiny house with two rooms. Up to now it has been just Mother, Grandmother, Oskar, little Sara and I, but we expect that they will move at least two more families in with us any day.

Last week we received a letter from Father with photo-copies of a very official looking document in Romanian and German, adorned and validated with various stamps and signatures.

Here is the translation of the document into English:

Embassy of the Republic of Chile

CERTIFICATE

The Chilean Embassy in Romania certifies herewith that Dr. Peilet Horowitz, owner of passport NO. 287 / p. issued by the Chilean Embassy in Romania, born on 17.04.1897 in Drohobycz Poland, is married to Perla Horowitz, nee Lanc-man, born on 03.18.1901 in Sosnowiec, Silesia and has 2 children, named Oskar, born on 01/10/1928 in Katowice, and Rudolph, born 24/02/1929 in Sosnowiec, resides in Bu-charest, at Sfintilor St. 9.

This certificate is issued to the above named individual for use as needed.

Bucharest, 2 March 1943

Father told us in his letter that he had concurrently sent a copy of the letter to the "Schutzamt", the Swiss Protec-tion Office in Berlin, which has the responsibility for protecting foreign nationals, requesting that they rescue his family.

Mother went to the Judenrat and showed it to Dr. Low-enstein, Moniek Meryn's deputy, who was very impressed.

The following day I was at home when Oskar came running, sobbing uncontrollably, tears streaming down his face, repeating, "Mother was arrested, Mother was arrested, she is gone".

We were despondent, not knowing what to do, wondering whether the document we received and the letter Father sent to the Swiss in Berlin provoked the German authorities. We didn't have to ponder long, as two militiamen appeared at our door and took us into custody. We spent a sleepless, restless night in the militia office resigned to the fact that if Mother is gone, we might as well go with her.

The following morning we were picked up by two uniformed Gestapo men driving a German style Jeep, and driven to Gestapo headquarters and from there to the Sosnowiec prison.

A German police officer started screaming at us shouting out commands I could not understand. He then stepped up to me and slapped me in the face so hard that I spun around facing the wall. Oskar who was facing the wall whispered to me that the German wanted us to face the wall and how come I did not understand it.

We were then placed in a tiny cell where a trustee clipped our hair very close.

The next morning the cell door opened and there was the police officer that slapped me, Dr. Lowenstein and Mother. The German was not shouting anymore and this time I understood every word he said. He spoke very politely addressing Mother as Madam and declaring that nothing serious happened to her boys except for the loss of hair, which after all will grow back. On that note we were released and went back to Srodula with Dr. Lowenstein.

Dr. Lowenstein explained that he had intervened with the German authorities, reminding them that as foreign nationals we were under the protection of the Swiss Red Cross and the Geneva Convention. Amazingly, this did the trick and we were released.

Two days after our release there was another roundup. The militia came out in force and made everyone assemble in an open field adjacent to the railroad yards. After hiding grandmother and Sara in the cellar we went to the appointed place, Mother clutching our Chilean Certificate.

This time there was no pretense about the Germans' intentions, as the cattle cars were right there, waiting to take on the human cargo. The Germans armed with machine guns surrounded the entire area and another selection begun. Dr. Lowenstein, upon seeing us, marched us over to the Gestapo man in charge, who was wielding, of all things, a carpet beater. Dr. L. explained that we were foreign nationals under the protection of the Swiss government and had documents to prove it. After examining our precious piece of paper the Gestapo man waved us on with his carpet beater, tapping Oskar and myself on the butt. What a touching demonstration of playfulness on the part of the Gestapo!

The news of our arrest and subsequent release spread like wildfire across the ghetto. So did the story of the miraculous lifesaving document in our possession. Since everyone knew that Father was not Chilean they assumed that he had very influential contacts in Romania and could produce such documents for others. Friends and acquaintances arrived in great numbers at our door asking for help and offering us their passport photos annotated with names, dates of birth etc. begging that we forward them to Father. Eventually, total strangers would show up and our collection of passport photos kept growing.

Upon returning home from the last selection we began to wonder how many more selections we would have to endure and whether we would survive them all.

The answer came this morning in the form of an official letter informing us that we would be transported to an "Ilag", Internment Camp for foreign nationals in Germany. We were to pack all our personal belongings (no limit on weight) and prepare to be picked up within two weeks.

Though still apprehensive and fearful that this is a ruse and we will wind up in Auschwitz we are trying to be of good cheer and are hoping for the best.

Mother is upbeat but she is constantly in tears over the impending separation from Grandma.

On that hopeful note I will sign off for now,

Your loving future Papa

May 2nd 1943

Dear Oscar and Emma,

We spent the last ten days packing all our essentials and after that was done we turned to household items, such as cutlery, feather bedding, etc. in the hope that we will be allowed to take it all, as well.

Using what little cash she had, Mother reached out to Mrs. Jaworska, our Polish countryside contact to secure some decent food for the journey. She bought some fresh peasant bread, ham, sausage, butter, cheese and smoked bacon. After so many years of deprivation I was ready to consume it all at one sitting, but Mother prevailed insisting that it was for the trip.

All the while we were constantly interrupted by a growing number of desperate souls arriving at our door forcing on us their passport photos annotated with personal details, and pleading for help.

The fateful day arrived on Thursday, April 18th. Shortly before noon a "Schupo" German police constable (not the dreaded SS or the Gestapo), arrived at the door announcing that he would be escorting us to an Internment Camp for women and children in Liebenau, Germany. He had all the train tickets and documents pertaining to our internment with him and told us that all we had to worry about was our luggage, he would see to every- thing else.

A gut-wrenching, tearful separation with Grandma followed. Amazingly, she was the most cheerful and happy of us all. Declaring that she was fully aware of her impending fate, she assured us that she would gladly accept it knowing that her daughter and grandsons will survive this terrible nightmare.

With heavy hearts we left the little house and followed our German escort to the edge of the ghetto, where, for the first time in four years we boarded a streetcar bound for the railway station.

As soon as we settled down the policeman, pointing at the yellow stars adorning our garments, said with contempt, "Remove that crap". Could it be, I wondered, that from all the Germans we had encountered since 1939, this one, who would be with us for the next two days, still had a shred of humanity in him?

On the way to the train we made a brief stop at the police station. There we met Mrs. Yanay, who was to join us on our trip to Liebenau. Mr. Yanay, her husband, immigrated to Palestine a British protectorate in the 1920's. Thus, both of them are British subjects and she merits the same protection as all enemy aliens.

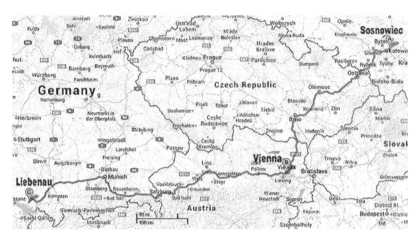

We boarded the night train for Vienna at about 7 pm. Mother went instantly into her prewar traveling mode, insisting that we remove our street shoes and replace them with slippers, so as to sleep better and keep our feet from swelling up. I thought it was silly, but I decided not to resist. Couldn't help, though, thinking about all those poor wretches packed into cattle cars, their foot- wear the least of their worries.

On arrival in Vienna at dawn we discovered that we had to change trains and RR terminals to continue our journey, with little time to spare. We must have made a strange sight running down the platform following the porter's cart with our entire luggage, wearing slippers, and clutching our street shoes in hand. After we changed into our street shoes inside the taxi, Mother never mentioned the slippers again.

The train from Vienna to Ulm was very crowded. In addition to the five of us there were four additional Germans in the compartment. Although Mrs. Yanay brought ample food for the trip, and offered to share it with us, Mother prepared lunch for all of us, including the German Policeman. That is when eyes started popping, mouths started watering and jaws began to drop on the faces of the German passengers.

Although there was hunger and shortages in Poland, it must have been a lot worse in the German Reich. Mother was in her element, and when it comes to gloating she cannot be bested. She started carrying on in her fluent German about how as foreign nationals we regularly receive the best victuals via Switzerland. Our German Policeman sat there silently munching on his ham and cheese sandwich and nodding as Mother spoke.

The train stopped in Ulm where we changed for a local and continued to our final destination in Tettnang. There we were picked up by a car and driven a short distance to the camp at Liebenau.

After our policeman delivered us to the camp and turned over the documents at the Guardhouse, the camp administration, which is organized and run by the women

The Schloss (castle)

internees, took charge of us. The head of the camp is Mrs. Froom, an elderly British lady who lives in the Schloss and whom we seldom see outside. Her deputy, Mrs. Walton is also British and unlike her superior she is a real busybody in the best sense of the word. She

Liebenau. The Schloss is in the background

seems to be everywhere, all the time. As soon as we arrived she assigned us to a large room with four beds in Joseph House, which we are sharing with Mrs. Yanay.

Before the war, Liebenau was a sanitarium/convent for the mentally retarded run by an order of Catholic nuns. Since the beginning of the war most of the mentally deficient had been euthanized on Hitler's orders. Coincidentally this made room for the internees.

The Camp is made up of several buildings. The Schloss (castle) is the oldest, dating back to the 17th Century. The internees occupy Joseph House and Clara House, and the back of Joseph house contains a one-room school. There is a large Catholic church with an adjacent convent for the nuns. A small building at the entrance to the camp contains the guardhouse. There are additional buildings outside the camp perimeter of undetermined use.

The nuns take care of the buildings and grounds and cook and serve meals to the internees in a large communal dining room. They are altogether a very unfriendly bunch. Moving around like crows in their black habits, they seem to be annoyed by all the internees, adults and children alike. Their Bavarian dialect is unintelligible and that is just as well, because I cannot imagine that they have a single kind word for any of us.

Mrs. Walton was explaining all this to us as she led us to lunch, which consisted of a watery soup made with cabbage and potatoes along with generous portions of bread and apples for dessert. Mrs. Walton assured us that we would not have to rely on this fare as a steady diet, as soon as we received our weekly Red Cross food packages.

We received the packages a week ago Monday, the same day we started school. Speaking of school, I have to finish my homework, now, so I'll tell you more about the packages and school in my next letter.

Your loving future Papa

June 30th, 1943

Dear Oscar and Emma,

In my last letter I promised to tell you about our school and the Red Cross packages. It happens that yesterday was the last day of school. No more classes until September.

The school is a single large classroom in Joseph's House. Our teacher is a lovely young Englishwoman, who does an incredible job of juggling the instruction of about a dozen kids of different ages and levels of educations. Though a lot of the material is already familiar to Oskar and me, we are eagerly repeating it in English with little difficulty. Frankly, I am amazed at how much we benefited from Ms. Matlis, our English tutor, back in Poland.

The weekly American Red Cross packages are simply unbelievable. A lot of the contents are unfamiliar on this side of the Atlantic. Among them are cans of corned beef, Spam, powdered milk, condensed milk, canned sardines and salmon, orange juice concentrate, cane sugar, cocoa powder, biscuits and powdered coffee. Each package contains five packs of cigarettes, which are removed from the children's packages by the women in charge of distribution. These ladies are probably very heavy smokers, themselves. The British Red Cross parcels are different and contain items more typical of the English diet. They are somewhat more modest in scope and variety, reflecting the greater wartime shortages in the British Isles.

Mother has been despairing over Grandma's situation and tried to get Father to somehow include her in our document. Though it is difficult to communicate openly because of the censorship, he made it clear that the document applied exclusively to his immediate family.

By now we have become accustomed to the camp routine; one of its high points being a daily two to three hour hike in the adjoining countryside. A single guard, usually the same elderly policeman, and a veteran of the First World War who is well into his sixties is our escort. He heads a column of unruly stragglers, both women and children stretching behind him for about ¼ mile. His favorite hiking companion is Miss Doreen, a beautiful, tall and leggy English music hall performer.

We walk through beautiful Bavarian countryside full of fertile fields and orchards against the backdrop of snow peaked Swiss Alps, which are only about 15 miles distant. It is hard to believe that there is a war going on and that we left behind us a place of such untold misery. Occasionally, the hikes are combined with apple picking which is done on a voluntary basis.

Miss Doreen is planning to put on a revue using all the talent she can muster in the camp. Because of my interest and past experience in art, I volunteered to assist in painting the scenery and my offer was readily accepted. I am very excited at the prospect of working in this new medium. The show will be staged in a large hall in the basement of the church. There is a raised platform at the far end of the hall, which will be used as a stage.

The area is very familiar to me for another reason. And that brings me to Lola a pretty, somewhat plump girl in our class. She is a few months older that I and has a passion for playing Hide-and-seek with the little kids. She usually makes sure that the little kids do the seeking and drags me to some very confined spaces behind the stage platform where she insists we remain hidden long after the game is over. Slowly, I am beginning to understand what is on her mind.

Meanwhile, after all the trauma, anxiety and fear that dominated our lives for the past four years, I am trying to get back to the business of being a teenager. Father sent me some watercolor pencils from Romania and I am busy painting. I am also busy with my favorite hobby of building rubber powered model airplanes. Noting my interest in the latter, our teacher showed me a series of "Teach Yourself" books in the school library pointing out that if I didn't find what I wanted in the library, I could request whatever title I wanted to be sent to me from England via the Red Cross. On examining the list of available titles I requested two books:"Teach Yourself to Fly", and "Teach Yourself Air Navigation".

That was about six weeks ago. Yesterday, Mrs. Walton told me that the books arrived at the Guard House and the Germans were wondering which internee was planning to flee the camp by flying out in a plane. I explained to her what my hobby was and that I wanted to learn how a real plane flies. She in turn told the Germans that the books were requested by a 14 year old boy who was curious to learn what made a plane fly and the books were turned over to me without further comment.

Coincidentally, Mother told me that she came across the aloof Mrs. Froom, head of the camp, who told Mother that of all the children in the camp Oscar and I were the best behaved, and she had every reason to be proud of us.

Things are looking up and our future looks brighter than it did since the Germans marched into Poland.

Until my next letter, with love,

Your future Papa

September 16th, 1943

Dear Oscar anEmma,

Summer is almost over and we are back at school, though we will not be here much longer as I will explain presently.

Our daily hikes frequently take us swimming to a nearby irrigation canal. The water is only about three feet deep, but deep enough for me to learn to swim all on my own. After first consulting a book on swimming at the school library I settled on learning to do the breast stroke which did not involve getting my head under water. The three-foot depth was just right to provide enough security when I lost cadence of the strokes or began to panic. After a month of trying, I can now venture into deeper water.Now that fall is here, another frequent hiking destination is one of the local orchards for apple picking.

This all sounds very idyllic and peaceful were it not for the nighttime air raids, which have become more frequent during the last few weeks. Although the bombing targets are military and industrial installations remote from Liebenau, we can hear the bombers close overhead as well as the anti-aircraft batteries, which are all around us. We dare not go out at night and we stay away from the windows. At daylight all the kids, me included run out and go treasure hunting for pieces of shrapnel from the AA guns.

Miss Doreen put on her revue at the end of August. It was a smashing success. Every internee attended including all the children and the German guards. It was great to see the show in its proper sequence and in costume for a change. As one of the artists working on the scenery I saw all the rehearsals and knew all the routines by heart. In fact one of the songs keeps following me constantly:

> There ain't no sense
> Sitting on the fence
> All by yourself in the moonlight
> There ain't no thrill
> By the water mill
> All by yourself in the moonlight
> Hes are made for shes
> And shes are made for hes
> Otherwise there'd be no family trees
> Even in the zoos
> They keep them there in twos
> Otherwise there'd be no little kangaroos

I wrote at the beginning of the letter that we will not be here much longer, and here's why.

As adolescent boys, Oskar and I are the oldest and biggest of the male children in the camp. Some of the ladies have complained to Mrs. Froom that we constitute an invasion of their privacy. Word of this also got to the German camp authorities. Their immediate reaction was that we should be transferred to a camp in Tittmoning for male enemy aliens and POW officers.

Understandably, Mother got very upset at the prospect of being separated from us. She pleaded with Mrs. Walton and Mrs. Froom, who managed to convince the German authorities that while we were too old to be in a women's camp, we were still under age and too young to be thrown in among adult male internees.

Thankfully, the Germans agreed to arrange for our transfer to a family camp in France. So here we are packing all over again. We expect to board a train for Vittel in France on Monday.

I will write to you again as soon as we settle in.

Sending you all my love

Your future Papa

January 14th, 1944

Dear Oscar and Emma,

It is three months since my last letter. Frankly, I have so

much to tell you that I literally don't know where to begin.

The hotel Nouvel

The train trip here was long and exhausting. We took a local from Tettnang to Ulm, then an express to Nancy in France and finally another local to Vittel, where we arrived late at night. Upon our arrival we were escorted directly to our as-

72

signed room at the Nouvel Hotel. In case you are wondering why a hotel in an internment camp, let me explain.

Vittel was a resort and spa famous for its mineral waters since the middle of the 19th century. After the Germans occupied France they converted it to a family camp for enemy aliens. It is divided into an American and British section which house about 2000 internees.

The footbridge

Both sections are fenced in and separated by a thoroughfare which runs right through it. A wooden footbridge over the thoroughfare connects the two sections. Our hotel, the Nouvel, is in the American section.

The casino and movie theater

Though the place is a bit seedy because of the war, and general neglect I am simply amazed at what the place has to offer. There is a beautiful

73

park in the British section with numerous clay tennis courts. The large casino building, which is located over

the mineral spring, houses a 400-seat movie theater.

French movies are shown on Saturdays and Sundays, with two showings of a new feature on each day. Although there are no subtitles and I don't under-

Miniature water color I painted for Mother's birthday 1944

stand French, both Oskar and I attend every showing on both days.

Our school is quite different from the one room school in Liebenau. We have regular classrooms with different grades and most of our teachers are American nuns, experienced in teaching. They are as different from the crows in Liebenau as the color of their habits, which is white, topped by a blue veil. They are cheerful and pleasant, and show a lot of affection and patience for the children. The best thing about the school is that I am with boys and girls my own age and I am making friends among them.

I spend a good deal of time with Jacek Kon who teaches me to play tennis and badminton. He is quite good at it,

74

but I catch on pretty quickly and give him a run for his money. Jacek looks a little like a younger version of the French actor Louis Jourdan, and he knows it. He also speaks fluent French and this gives him even more reason to put on airs. No wonder, though, as his deceased grandfather, Prof. Moses Schorr was the chief reform rabbi in Poland, a prominent teacher and scholar, as well as a member of the Polish senate. Jacek is here with his two younger brothers, Peter and Stefan, as well as his mother and grandmother. They were saved from doom in the Warsaw ghetto by virtue of documents similar to ours, except for their origin, which is Nicaragua.

A couple of girls in my class are also worth mentioning. My favorite is Lusia also from Poland, here with her parents holding a legitimate Brazilian passport. My attempts to get her to notice me are futile and she just keeps ignoring me. Then there is Micheline who was orphaned during the Spanish civil war and was adopted by a British couple. A dark beauty with penetrating black eyes, she is generally regarded as the most beautiful young girl in the camp. She is also one of the worst students in our class. Somehow, Micheline seems to be attracted to me, as she keeps popping up wherever I happen to be, trying to attract my attention. With my mind on Lusia, I ignore her and avoid her advances. The best I could muster during a recent encounter was to tell Micheline to concentrate on her studies.

Speaking of studies, Oskar is 16 today and does not attend the school having completed all the material offered by the curriculum. Instead, he is taking private lessons in Latin from Captain Shillito who is a POW Anglican British Army chaplain.

I should also mention Miss Harris, a middle aged English lady who befriended Mother and takes her for a daily walk around the park. I think this is just dandy, as Miss Harris speaks only English and Mother is gradually picking up the basics of the language.

We are getting our American Red Cross packages punctually every Friday, except that here, the cigarettes are not removed from Oskar's and my packages. Since American cigarettes are the best currency for trading both inside the camp and outside and we do not smoke, we are quite well off by camp standards. From time to time we receive packages with clothing, especially at the onset of winter.

Every Saturday evening there is a dance at the Nouvel Hotel ballroom. It is always very popular with young men and women from both sides of the camp. Though I don't dance I attend all the dances just to listen to the music. The music comes from a single upright piano and an English gentleman whose magic fingers play the most wonderful jazz I have ever heard.

The camp commandant, a Wehrmacht officer known by his first name, Stefan, stays pretty much out of the internee's hair. His frequent companion is Miss Justo, a young German-Jewish woman with a Brazilian passport, buckteeth and a receding chin. As if her unattractive appearance were not enough to make her repulsive, her penchant for kissing up to the German makes sure of that.

Before I close for today, I must tell you about what happened in the last few days.

The first incident of a minor, but personal nature was a badminton game I arranged to play against Lusia and Micheline at the same time. In this odd triangle I played against a girl whose attention I was seeking and a girl who was seeking my attention. Notably, this was the only "date" I had with either of them so far.

The second incident was the recent arrival of some 300 Jews from the Warsaw ghetto, all bearing South American, primarily Paraguayan documents. They are all very orthodox, clad in the traditional black kaftans and black fedoras, complete with beards and side-curls. At least forty of them shared the last name, Rapaport.

The German camp authorities placed them all at the Providence a small hotel about a block distant from ours. The new arrivals promptly established a synagogue with scheduled daily prayers and generally conducted themselves as if the Germans were on another planet. We were all wondering if their papers were genuine, though rumor had it that the entire group was related to a Rabbi Rapaport who lived in Switzerland and somehow got them these papers.

After living through and surviving the horrors of the ghetto and deportations in Poland, I can't help wishing that the new arrivals kept a lower profile and stopped poking their fingers in the Nazis eyes. Could they be tempting fate?

Very anxiously,

Your loving future Papa

June 7th, 1944

Dear Oscar and Emma,

I did not write to you in six months because some of the recent events in Vittel brought back bitter memories of the deportations in Sosnowiec, which I thought we had left behind.

Yet here I am, excited and elated beyond belief by the news that the Allies landed on the beaches of Normandy at dawn yesterday. Think of it! That is just about 500 kilometers, as the crow flies, from Vittel.

Since I cannot read French, we get our news from the "Pariser Zeitung", a German language paper published in Paris. It is full of headlines about this momentous event with stories about how the Wehrmacht is repulsing the Yanks and the Tommies, and pushing them back into the English Channel. Of course I know better. The Jerries are famous for misleading battle reports since they were pushed out of Stalingrad, in 1943, when the phrase "planmäßig geräumt" (strategic withdrawal) first appeared.

When I last wrote you speculating that the orthodox Jews in Hotel Providence may be tempting fate, my words were prophetic. Apparently the Germans began to suspect the authenticity of the South American citizenship documents held by so many Jews in Vittel.

Rumor had it that the suspicions were fueled by one shady character. Mr. Koenig, is a small weasel of a man, bald headed, sporting a Hitler mustache and strutting around the camp in his fur-lined jacket and black riding boots, reminiscent of the Jewish militia in Sosnowiec. He arrived in Vittel with the last transport from Warsaw and apparently has South American documents himself. He keeps very much to himself and is occasionally seen visiting the Commandant's office.

Late last January a Gestapo delegation arrived from Berlin issuing a notice that all holders of South American papers, were to appear by scheduled appointment at the Commandant's office. This, of course included us.

Mother went to the meeting at the designated time and returned about a half hour later. She told us that the Gestapo men were very polite, but kept grilling her as to how she obtained the documents, were they genuine, how much money she paid for them, etc. She calmly and categorically responded that she did not buy the documents and did not ask for them, that she was a Polish subject and had the documents because she was married to a subject of Chile. Although she maintained her composure during the interview she was quite shaken upon her return.

Toward the end of March the ax fell and about 300 Jews with those ill-fated papers were transferred to Hotel Beau Site, outside the camp and placed under armed guard. Thankfully, we were not among them. My friend Jacek Kon with his two brothers, his mother and grandma had to go. So did Mother's friend, Fran Zucker with her family.

Most of the unfortunates were packed into trains and transported in two groups, one in April and one in May to a transit camp at Drancy, outside of Paris. From there they were sent east to "parts unknown", which we knew was Auschwitz.

Very few of the 300 managed to stay behind. Jacek's grandmother, Mrs. Schorr committed suicide by swallowing poison and his mother jumped out of the hotel window, suffering severe injuries, which put her in the hospital. The boys were left alone and were not included in the transport. Mrs. Zucker suffered a heart attack even as her husband and two children were deported, and was saved by going to the hospital.

To think that these poor souls were murdered during the last gasps of the Nazi Empire makes it particularly painful. Now that the invasion is underway, we can assume that the few who evaded the last transport, my friend, Jacek, among them will be spared.

This is another one of those rare bittersweet periods that I have experienced since 1939. Payback time is near!

With love and devotion,

Your future Papa

September 24th, 1944

Dear Oscar and Emma,

After the Allies landing in June I got a map of France and tacked it on the wall above my bed. Using color map pins I daily updated the battle lines on my map. Though my only source of information from the front was the German Pariser Zeitung, which notoriously exaggerated the news in favor of the Germans, the steady, relentless progress of the Allies was still very obvious.

Although at first the going was quite tough and the Allies fought very hard for the beachheads, and the hedge-rows, gradually they started pushing the Germans back and by mid-July I kept moving my pins daily in our direction.

While the battles in Normandy and beyond are on the ground, the daily over flight of American Flying Fortresses on the way to Germany were something to behold. The formations are flying at 35,000 to 40,000 feet and they are so vast that it often takes them a whole hour to fly by.

By August 19th the Yanks and the Free French forces reached Paris. The battle for Paris lasted nearly a week and we no longer got our news from the Pariser Zeitung. On August 25th news reached us that General de Gaulle marched triumphantly into Paris and the city was liberated.

Toward the end of August we began to watch Stefan and his guards very closely, for signs of imminent departure. By Wednesday the 30th all the guards were gone and the only sign of German presence was Stefan's olive drab Citroen sedan parked outside his office. All through the following night we could hear the ceaseless grinding of the Citroen starter motor with the engine stubbornly refusing to fire. By morning the car and Stefan were gone. We later heard that some of the French FFI (underground forces) poured sugar into his gas tank, which literally gummed up the works.

On the morning of September 3rd a small detachment of the FFI triumphantly arrived outside the camp below the footbridge and set up a very large machine gun on the corner of the street, to loud cheers and applause of the internees.

By noon the machine gun was gone as word reached the FFI guys that a substantial number of German forces were engaged in their "strategic withdrawal" and would be coming through. This charade went on for a week with the machine gun appearing and vanishing as more Germans were fleeing. To my great disappointment the FFI never fired at the retreating Germans. On Sunday morning, September 10th an American Jeep followed by a Sherman tank drove into Vittel and stopped below the footbridge. I can still hear the thunderous cheering that followed. The cheering turned into a roar at the sight of a couple of GI's escorting some two dozen German soldiers with their hands high up over their heads. The roar turned into side-splitting laughter when one of the Germans came into view without his pants on. Sieg Heil, indeed!

The next day General Leclerc with his Free French army marched in and officially liberated Vittel. For us the war was over.

The gates of the camp were suddenly open and we are free to go anywhere we please. It is exciting to meet and mix with GI's from all parts of the US. They were equally thrilled to meet so many English-speaking civilians. All generous to a fault they shower us, especially the youngsters, with candy and chewing gum.

The opportunity to interact with so many "real Americans" is simply overwhelming. I am learning a lot of new English expressions and phrases and am mostly impressed by their constant swearing and the use of "goddam". Everything is goddam this, or goddam that, and while I refrain from using the obviously foul and insulting words, I pepper my daily speech with friends and strangers alike with a more benign phrase which includes "goddam". Still, I am baffled and cannot understand why anyone would want to suck a rooster.

No more French movies on weekends. Instead, the US Army installed a 16 mm projector in the aisle of the theater and for the first time in my life I saw an American movie, "Anthony Adverse", without subtitles. The last time I saw an American film before that, was as a small boy in Sosnowiec starring my true love, Shirley Temple.

Mother and I with US Army Col. Winkelman below the footbridge, Sept 1944

On one occasion Mother volunteered to help out at a nearby field hospital where we met Colonel Winkelman, a doctor from New York.

For some strange reason I got very embarrassed when she tried to help a wounded soldier wash his arm. When I asked her to stop doing it she got very angry with me. To this day I cannot understand what made me feel that way.

86

A few days after the liberation Oskar came home very excited. He along with a crowd of people was filmed by a newsreel cameraman from "The March of Time". I won-

Oskar appears in a "March of Time" documentary. Sept. 1944

der if he will wind up on the silver screen.

Joyfully,

Your loving future Papa

May 10th 1945

Dear Oscar and Emma,

Great news! Last week Germany surrendered uncondi-
tionally to the Allied forces shortly after Hitler committed
suicide. The war in Europe is over. Sorry I did not write to
you sooner, but we have been on the move and time just
flew by. We are now in La Bourboule since last Novem-

ber. It is a small resort town in the Massif Central Mountains in central France.

Shortly after the liberation most of the Brits were sent back to England, and the Americans back to the States.

A lot of other people, we included, are in a sort of limbo, with no immediate destination to go to.

We have all been transferred to a DP (Displaced Persons) camp here, in La Bourboule. This is not a camp in the strict sense of the word, as we are living in a very nice hotel. There are no fences or gates and we are free to go as we please. There are no Red Cross packages either, but we get three meals a day in the hotel dining room. We also get a ration of one bottle of red table wine, each, per week. I indulge myself by taking regular swigs from my bottle.

The food is so-so with one notable negative exception: the chef's favorite is lentil soup, which he serves at least three times per week. Needless to say, we've just about had it with lentil soup and if I never taste it again it will be too soon.

US Army Captain Fox administers the DP camp. Shortly after arriving here, I applied for a job in the

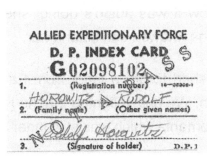

My ID card

office and Captain Fox took me on as a messenger-errand boy. This is an unpaid position except for the generous amount of chewing gum and candy dispensed by the GI's in the office. Much to my disgust, the chinless Miss Justo is also here. She was hired by the Captain to do some office work. Of course, she is kissing up to Capt. Fox just as she did with Stefan, the Nazi in Vittel. I get furious when I see her riding around in a jeep with Capt. Fox and I wish I had the courage to tell the Captain what she is all about.

Unfortunately my job was very short lived. One of the GI's showed me how to work the clutch and shift gears in the jeep without my actually getting behind the wheel. One day, I decided to put his lesson into practice, and while the jeep was parked behind the office, I drove it back and forth about 10 feet, in forward and reverse till I got the hang of it.

The next morning, exactly two weeks after I was hired Capt. Fox called me into his office and taught me a new American phrase I have never heard before, "You drove the jeep. You're fired!" I know it was Justo's doing; she saw me drive the jeep and she knows I can't stand her.

In February we were astonished to get a letter from Father who is now in Jerusalem. We are delighted that he is in Palestine and got out of Romania which was still under the Nazi boot at the time he left. He wrote that he is doing everything possible to get us to join him there.

Now that we come in daily contact with the locals around town I realize that the Saturday and Sunday afternoons I spent watching French movies in Vittel are paying off. I find that I can communicate reasonably well with the natives. This is very useful as I met Alain, a French boy who is my age and has the same passion for model airplanes as I do. He is way ahead of me, though; he has a tiny one cylinder gasoline engine with a propeller which he keeps testing on his workbench. He has yet to build a model airplane and fly it with this engine.

Back in February Alain invited me to go skiing with him, which I eagerly accepted. He let me borrow an extra pair of skis boots and poles, which belong to his older sister. We took a bus to Mont Dore, which is a few miles distant from La Bourboule and has some great ski terrain. This was my second time on skis ever, but I am looking forward to doing a lot more of it in future.

Alain has a subscription to a French youth weekly, "Le Coq Hardi" which he generously passes on to me after reading it. One of the recent issues announced a drawing competition, which called for a depiction of the liberation of the City of Strasbourg. I decided to enter it and for the past two weeks I have been laboring on a very detailed pen and ink drawing depicting the cathedral of

Strasbourg with a giant figure of a G I straddling the monument. I am very proud of my artwork and hope to win the competition. I will be sending it in tomorrow. Too bad I cannot make a copy of the drawing for my record.

So long for now,

Your devoted future Papa

July 20th, 1945

Dear Oscar and Emma,

Just a short note to bring you up to date on what happened since I last wrote to you in May.

After a long, arduous six-year separation we were reunited yesterday with Father. I am writing from a hotel room in Haifa, as we are waiting to take a train to Jerusalem later this afternoon.

The Mataroa

A week ago we took a train from La Bourboule to Marseille and boarded a small ship, which took us to Naples. There we transferred to the Mataroa, a much larger vessel for the trip to Haifa. The ship was packed with survivors of concentration camps bearing tattooed serial numbers on their forearms. Most of them were young men and boys with a smaller number of women.

The women were placed in comfortable cabins, while all the men were crowded into a giant hold and given a hammock to sleep in. If this is how sailors slept in the old days, I don't know how they got any rest at all.

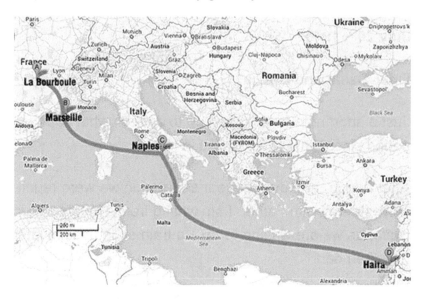

I had an odd feeling of guilt among all these camp survivors and almost felt ashamed for not having a number on my forearm. "Was I getting away with something?" I thought. I know my feelings were irrational, for surely those poor souls did not carry their tattoos as a mark of heroism or distinction and would have happily traded places with me. After all it was pure luck that kept us from their fate or worse.

We landed in Haifa on July 15th and were transported by bus to Atlit, a transit camp for illegal immigrants to Palestine. Palestine has been a British protectorate since the breakup of the Ottoman Empire after the end of World War I. The Brits are restricting the unlimited immigration of Jews to Palestine in order to placate the Arab population.

So here we are again, fenced in by the people who are supposed to be our saviors. This time our confinement is very brief. Within the hour we caught a glimpse of Father approaching the fence where we were waiting. His first words were, "Which one of you is which?" for he couldn't distinguish between Oskar and myself after six years.

Thankfully, about an hour later we were released into his arms and a tearful reunion. Father has been working in a Polish clinic, which took care of a large number of Polish officers and their families who fled the Germans and were scattered all over. Palestine was one of the places where they took refuge. As a former Polish officer, Father had no difficulty in getting us out.

Catching up on our respective histories after a six year separation is a formidable task but one of the first things we had to find out was how Father obtained the Chilean citizenship which saved us from certain doom. Mother raised this question as soon as we boarded the bus for Haifa. Father explained that he did not have a Chilean citizenship. The Chilean government had an agreement with the Polish government in exile to issue passports to Polish citizens in Romania who desired to travel to other countries and had no document to be validated with an appropriate visa. The passport clearly indicated its purpose and the bearer's Polish citizenship. Father had us included in the passport, and then sent us photocopies of all the pages except the one indicating his citizenship. Then, with the assistance of a grateful patient who was an official in the Romanian Foreign Ministry he obtained a very official looking document festooned with stamps and signatures declaring that he was the bearer of Chilean passport number so and so and has a wife and children included in the passport, etc. all of which was absolutely true and quite enough to fool the Nazis into believing that possession of the Passport clearly implied citizenship. Additionally he sent letters and a telegram to the Swiss Embassy "Schutzamt" in Berlin, the office responsible for protecting enemy aliens, requesting that they protect his wife and children. While it wasn't a forgery, it was a perfect scam and it fooled the Nazis.

After spending the night at a hotel in Haifa we are off as a family to start a new life.

So long for now with love and kisses

Your future Papa

September 10th 1946

Dear Oscar and Emma,

It is over a year since I last wrote to you but I intend to bring you fully up to date before I finish this letter.

When we arrived in Jerusalem last year in July our feeling of elation at being reunited at last, was thoroughly dampened upon entering Father's living quarters. He was renting a small room with a double bed, a small wardrobe and hardly a hint of furniture. He borrowed a mattress from the landlord for Oskar and me to sleep on. With the mattress spread on the floor there was almost no room to move around.

Father explained patiently that in the few months since he arrived in Palestine his first and only priority was to get us to join him. Moreover, the housing situation was very dire; there were few rentals available and decent apartments were usually offered for sale at exorbitant prices. For the moment his income at the Polish clinic was insufficient to undertake the burden of a major pur- chase.

Furthermore, he had no intention for us to make our permanent home there. Instead, he felt that we should immigrate to the USA, as Oskar and I would have much better opportunities there.

In the meantime, using the good offices of the Polish clinic he arranged a two-week vacation rental for us in an Arab village close to Jerusalem. This was a vacation like none I experienced before. The place was hot, arid and dusty. Not even remotely reminiscent of the farmhouses we vacationed in before the war. The only greenery was the vast olive grove surrounding the village on all sides, where each olive tree was a unique piece of sculpture. Despite that we enjoyed the place very much and got a well-deserved rest. Our Arab landlord assuming we belonged to the Polish contingent was hospitable to a fault. Father visited frequently during our stay.

Upon returning to Jerusalem Father arranged for Oskar and me to spend a couple of weeks in a youth kibbutz, while he sought better accommodations.

The time in the kibbutz was a complete bust. It reminded me of the Boy Scout camp we went to in July 1939. There was a lot of singing of patriotic Hebrew songs and indoctrination into the Zionist ideal. The one redeeming feature about the place was the animals. They had donkeys, cows, goats, horses and all sorts of fowl. Working with and among them did not involve any idealism and I enjoyed it thoroughly. When asked at the end of two weeks for an evaluation of the place and which of the activities appealed to me most, my simple answer was, "The animals." I went home on the following day.

Father and Mother were not too disappointed that we did not make it in the kibbutz. They both had higher aspirations for both of us. By now they had a slightly larger apartment, so we did not have to sleep on the floor.

In our absence, Father registered all of us at the American Consulate for immigration to America. The bad news was that the Polish quota was oversubscribed, and we would have to wait four to five years for our number to come up.

Since continuing and completing our studies was very important, Oskar, the self-disciplined scholar would stay at home in Jerusalem and continue his studies there, and I would go away to a boarding school to learn a trade.

The school they had in mind is located in the northern town of Tzfat and trained young men in making surgical instruments. Since I was skillful and adept at using my hands Mother and Father believed this would be a good path for me to take. The Youth Resettlement Office was to provide the wherewithal for my enrollment.

In the meanwhile the Polish clinic and the Polish contingent in Jerusalem were going to move to Iran and England. Father was asked to join them together with us. Since this would interfere with our education and meant more dislocation and wandering, he declined the offer. Instead he accepted a position at the Kupat Cholim (National Health Service) in Haifa. He made a down payment on a new apartment in Haifa and they made the move last year, just about the time I left for Tzfat.

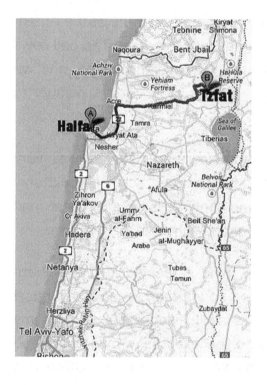

Tzfat or Safed is an ancient town located in the hills of Galilee. It is famous for an uninterrupted Jewish presence since before the days of ancient Rome. The school is located high up on a hill and has an enrollment of both local boys and the boarders. The boarding residence is located a few blocks down a steep hill from the school.

The principal of the boarding house is Shalom Weinstein assisted by his wife Elisheva. There are two additional staff women who cook, clean and wash. Shalom also teaches Hebrew and Hebrew literature at the school. The Weinsteins are in their late thirties. They both came to Palestine before the war from Germany. Though they are fluent in Hebrew, when alone, I sometimes overhear them conversing in German.

There are about 20 boys in residence. They come from all over Europe and range in age from 13 to 17. Many of them are Holocaust survivors, and a few bear the tattooed serial number on their forearms. I share a room with two boys my age, Eric (Tzvi) Rosenberg, and Wolfie (Zeev) Chlamtatch. Eric went to England from Germany with the Kinder-transport in the spring of 1939. Wolfie with his parents as well as Eric's parents were denied entry into Palestine by the British in early

I am on the far right, Wolfie is standing 2nd from the right, Shalom is next, Eric is standing 3rd from the left

101

1940, and were exiled to the island of Mauritius for the duration of the war. Both Eric and Wolfie are my best friends.

Although we are strongly encouraged to use our Hebrew names – mine is Rafael – I resent it but cannot avoid it. Likewise, the Weinsteins as well as some of the other boys in the house frown upon my conversing with my friends in English. I feel I am being indoctrinated against my will into becoming a loyal subject of the Jewish homeland. I know that most teenagers rebel against the authority of their parents. In their absence I rebel against the Weinsteins. Though I don't share this with anyone here, I know that sooner or later I will go to America and leave all this nonsense behind me.

School is different; I enjoy it very much. We spend mornings on academic subjects and afternoons in the shop. Shop is particularly rewarding. I learn to use various hand tools for working with metal as well as machine tools including, a drill press, a lathe and a shaper. My first semester assignment is to make a surgical pair of scissors from scratch using hand tools and a raw, flat piece of steel.

Head of shop is Mr. Eckstein, a precision toolmaker who like most of the staff hails from Germany. Shop and drafting are my favorite subjects and I excel in both, getting A's and A+'s in them routinely.

Mr. Eckstein singled me out as his favorite using my work as an example for the other students. I really hate this, as being a "teacher's pet" brings on resentment and teasing from other students.

I go home to Haifa whenever there is a holiday. Last time I was there, Oskar offered to enroll me and pay for a preparatory correspondence course for the London University Matriculation (equivalent of a High School Diploma) if I commit myself to do the studying. Oskar has a job and is earning money while he is studying for the same examination, which he plans to take in January. I know that with a full time school schedule and the extra chores in the house it will be difficult for me but I am committed to do it.

Speaking of extra chores, all the boys are obliged to do some work in the house after school. I volunteered to pitch in, in the sewing room. This involves repairing the boys' torn uniforms on a foot-operated sewing machine. I learned to operate the sewing machine very quickly, and I find this work much more agreeable than cleaning up the kitchen.

The correspondence course material including all the textbooks and lessons arrived in a big package from Cairo at the beginning of last month. I plunged into it at once and established a routine of at least two hours of studies per night before going to sleep. Twice a week I mail my completed papers to my proctor in Cairo. These are returned corrected and graded a week later. I know I should feel over worked, but the truth is I am enjoying myself too much to consider my studies a burden.

I have a hunch that the Weinsteins are not too keen on my English studies. I seriously doubt that he will ever bring it out in the open. After all Shalom would fail as an educator if he tried to dissuade a student from studying whatever he chooses. Unfortunately, the Brits are regarded as the enemy here, because of their policy of restricting Jewish immigration into Palestine. Matter of fact Jewish terrorists blew up the King David Hotel in Jerusalem last July killing many British officers billeted there. I find it difficult to share those sentiments after all the acts of kindness we experienced from the Brits while in Liebenau and Vittel.

It is getting very late and I took time out from my evening studies to write this letter to you, so I will close for now,

With love,

Your future Papa.

November 11ᵗʰ 1947

Dear Oscar and Emma,

Today is Armistice Day a holiday celebrated around the world to commemorate the end of World War I and to promote peace. Here in Palestine we are preparing for war.

But I am getting ahead of myself, as I owe you an update since my last letter in September a year ago. The reason for my silence is that nothing too momentous happened worth writing about. Last September I completed my correspondence course, and I am simply amazed at how much free time I have gained as a result.

I spend most of my free time with my friends Eric and Wolfie, reading English novels and Wolfie's Reader's Digest, and learning to dance. Eric who learned to dance in England is my dance teacher. He is a whiz at the jitterbug, and has a mastery of the fox trot and the English waltz. We tune the radio in to a British Army station in Jerusalem, which plays excellent jazz music. Needless to say Shalom frowns on this activity, as he does on my other pursuits.

On occasion we buy a bottle or two of red wine, sneak up on the roof after lights out and have a jolly old time downing the wine while telling dirty jokes and fantasizing about girls. Another more benign pastime is strolling on the main street and ogling Ruth, the prettiest girl in town whom we have nicknamed "Cutie".

Speaking of strolling, we only go as far as the top of the hill on the main drag, as that is the beginning of the Arab quarter. Going beyond that point invariably invites rock throwing from the Arab boys. Another presence in the street is the ubiquitous British police patrols, who stroll back and forth in pairs.

Two weeks ago Eric and I were suddenly arrested during our walk on suspicion of vandalizing one of the police vehicles. The fact that we denied the charges in fluent English aroused even more suspicion. After several hours in the pen, Shalom had us released after explaining that as boarders in the school under constant supervision, we could not possible have been the culprits.

While resentment against the British grows because of their anti-immigration policy, the Arabs are getting increasingly restless and belligerent, even as the United Nations is debating the future of Palestine.

As the unrest is growing, the boarding school added a new discipline to our curriculum. Every Sunday afternoon we spend two hours in "Kapap" training. Kapap is a martial art involving fighting with sticks. I find it stupid and hate every minute of it just as much as I hate my potential involvement in another war. The notion of a Jewish State always reminds me of an item I read in one of Wolfie's Readers Digests. In it Charlie Chaplin was quoted as saying that sending all the Jews to Palestine makes as much sense as sending all the Catholics to Rome.

In ten days I am going home for a weekend. I wish I could stay there and not have to come back to Kapap and all the patriotic nonsense I have to put up with here, in Tzfat. If only we could leave for America now.

Sending you all my love,

Your future Papa

February 10th, 1948

Dear Oscar and Emma,

It is some time since I wrote to you last. I am writing this letter from a jail cell at the notorious Pawiak prison in Warsaw, Poland. This is my third time in jail and I am not even eighteen. There are two other grown men here, with me. Oskar is in another cell.

Let me start where I left off -- in Palestine, in November of last year. The United Nations General Assembly ratified the partition of Palestine; the Jews accepted it and the Arabs prepared for war.

In early December I went home to Haifa to visit Mother and Father for a weekend, from the trade school in Tzfat. After the long suffering during the war years and the trauma it brought to our small surviving family, your great grandparents didn't want Oskar and me to be exposed to more danger, especially since we never intended to stay in Palestine, and were waiting for our visas for the USA. I was not going back to Tzfat.

We started laying plans for Oskar's and my departure. Mother had a cousin, Regina, who survived the camps and was living in Munich, Germany. It was decided that Oskar and I would go to Munich and stay with her until our immigration quota numbers come up and then proceed to America. Mother and Dad would go to the US from Haifa.

As we had no way of getting directly to Germany, we would obtain Polish passports, buy air passage to Warsaw and somehow, en route make our way to Munich. Since this was a fairly expensive proposition for Mother and Dad, we were cautioned to watch our resources carefully. I was selected to go to the Polish Consulate in Tel-Aviv, with our birth certificates and obtain the passports. I stayed at the apartment of a family friend, Lolek, a big fat guy with an excellent selection of French Cognac in his wardrobe, from which I took generous swigs in his absence.

On my second day in Tel-Aviv I presented myself at the consulate to fill out the applications. The passport official gave me a choice of two documents, one valid for general travel at £10.00 each, and the other for return to Poland only, at £5.00 each. Wary of my budget I selected the cheaper option. A few days later, in mid-December I went back to the consulate and picked up the passports and took a bus back to Haifa.

The next stage of planning was to prepare us for the journey. Though both of us were still teenagers we couldn't venture out into the big world looking like ones. Thus Mother took us shopping and we left the man's store wearing identical brown herringbone tweed top-coats with matching brown fedoras. Grown up, indeed, except that we looked more like a grown-up version of our 2½ and 3½-year-old selves wearing identical blue wool coats and berets going for a walk with our nanny in Sosnowiec.

Next came the most exciting part: booking our first ever airplane flight, to Warsaw with a short layover in Rome and a week layover in Prague, Czechoslovakia. Of course we would attempt to get to Munich from Rome or Prague with no intention of going to Communist Poland. The flight was scheduled to leave at the beginning of February, which left us about 6 weeks for the final prepa-rations.

The final phase of the plan was to provide us with emer-gency funds for the trip until we arrive and settle in Mu-nich. Mother and Dad scraped up $300, which is a lot of money in Palestine, and a Midas' fortune in post war Eu-rope. Mother decided that the best way to keep the money secure and safe was to change it all into singles and conceal $150, in each of our garments. She stitched them neatly into our trouser cuffs, belts and any other places where the fabric was thick or doubled.

It looked like we were all set, and all we had to do is wait for our February departure.

Shortly after the New Year, I was walking along a main street in Haifa, when I ran into a friend of Oskar's who asked me,

"Weren't you taking a correspondence course for the London University Matriculation exam?"

He knew about it from Oskar who completed his Matriculation, was working and paying for my correspondence course.

"Of course", I answered in the affirmative.

"Don't you know that the exams are taking place at this very minute at the gymnasium of Technion University? They must be half way through by now."

My jaw dropped. After three years of self-study, in my free time, after regular school hours I was going to miss the thing I wanted most. The London Matriculation, an open door to any university in the world. I raced to the Technion, which was only a few blocks away and arrived sweaty, about an hour after the exams papers were handed out. The English exam was in progress and I had two hours left to complete it. Evidently, my notice for the exam was sent to the school in Tzfat, which I had left in November. For the next three days I had nothing else on my mind but to be at the Technion an hour before the start of each examination. This debacle gave me a lot of anxiety and I was absolutely sure that I failed.

The rest of January passed quickly and soon we were in Lydda embarking a 4-engine propeller driven, British airliner for Prague with a 3-hour stop in Rome. Now this was exciting! Up in the air! For the moment we took it all in, thrilled at flying and being on our own.

Reality soon set in when we landed in Rome. As we

stepped into the terminal it became painfully obvious that we could not get off the plane there. The rapid staccato of the Italian language, everything appearing so foreign and forbidding made us cower. With little time left to board the plane, we decided to continue to Prague and try our luck there.

We arrived in Prague late in the afternoon. After checking into the hotel we went for a long walk along the main commercial district past spacious squares and plazas and parks. We had a reservation to continue to Warsaw the following week via the Polish airline, LOT. It is time to make our way to Munich.

The next morning we went to the Prague Jewish Community Bureau for assistance. After a long wait in crowded waiting room, we explained to the stern looking woman at the desk that we are trying to get to America by way of Munich. Could she help us?

"Where did you come from?" she asked.

"From Palestine", I answered.

She gazed speechless, and astounded and finally said,

""Do you see the throng of people, all Holocaust survivors, in this room? They are all dying to get to Palestine to create a Jewish Homeland. And you two, young able bodied men leave there to go to America? Aren't you ashamed? Get out of here this instant!"

As we were leaving, a short, slight man named Sam approached and addressed me in Polish saying that he heard the entire conversation and asked us to follow him. In the street he indicated that he, too, had left Pales- tine a short time ago and was also on his way to relatives in the USA.

"Do you have any traveling documents and money?" he asked,

I replied that we had Polish passports and had some money in US$.

He then took us to the travel office where he got passage to Belgium, a country, which was at the time very liberal in issuing visas to war refugees. The clerk at the travel agency took one look at the passport and told us that he could sell us train ticket for Brussels, but that we would never get a visa from any country as our documents were clearly valid only for return to Poland.

OOPS! That was one giant crack in the pavement I just stepped on.

As we were leaving, Sam, who now felt sorry for us, offered another suggestion. Apparently, all those throngs of people in the community office were crossing the border to Germany without any papers, by paying off the border guards. Since we were pariahs in the Prague office he told me there was another community bureau closer to the border, in Karlovy Vary (Carlsbad), a world-renowned spa since the 19th century, popular with the rich and famous and world aristocracy. This time, he suggested don't tell them the truth, just say that you came from Poland and you are trying to get to Palestine.

We boarded a train, and reached our destination late in the evening. Though this was winter in post-war Europe,

the empty hotel we checked into was something to behold. The stunning suite we were led to could host a party of 100 with room to spare and it cost literally pennies to rent. Though thrilled like kids in a candy store, we had to focus on our immediate problem. In the morning, we located the local Jewish Community Bureau, which was deserted, except for one bespectacled little, old man behind a desk. When I told him our newly minted story, he said that we were in the wrong place and that the Prague office took care of those matters. Asking why we didn't go there, my answer was that this was the advice given to us on the way.

"Well, no point doubling back to Prague", he offered, "The border crossing is at Aš, here's the address you should go to, ask for Bolek, he is a member of the Haganah, he will help you".

With that we left, checked out of the hotel and caught a train for Aš. On arrival early that evening, we found Bolek who was a strapping big fellow in his late 20's with an equally imposing assistant. We told him our story and he started interrogating us in Polish, as to why we didn't stop in Prague, how we got there from Poland, and a lot more uncomfortable questions. Then turning to his companion he started to discuss our case with obvious skepticism, in Hebrew! Of course, unaware that we were both fluent in that language, they commented about our attire; clad in those ridiculous matching herringbone topcoats and brown fedoras, we looked nothing like the refugees they were used to assisting across the border to Germany.

They decided to call their bosses at the Prague Community Bureau the next morning for advice. Turning to us in

Polish they offered us lodging for the night promising to deal with our case on the following day. It looked like our goose was cooked. Surely, the Prague lady would identify us instantly from his description. They called in a man who was to take us to our room for the night. On the way there, we asked him to stop at a bathroom. As he waited for us outside, we climbed out the window and ran as fast as our legs would carry us for the train station, caught the first train for Prague, resigned to go back to Poland. At noon on the following day we collected what little luggage we left at the hotel and boarded a Polish LOT DC-3 for Warsaw.

On the flight we met a fellow in his twenties named Lutek who had a similar story to ours; he too was a survivor, going from Palestine to Poland with no ultimate destination, merely unwilling to get into another war.

On arrival at the Okęcie airport we went immediately through passport and customs check. The terminal was full of uniformed Polish soldiers who performed the searches of the new arrivals. Oscar was taken into a private cubicle for a strip search and within minutes the soldier emerged triumphantly waving a couple of dollar bills yelling at his companion, "Get the other one, they are full of contraband, they're currency manipulators!". Using a razor blade he opened every stitch that Mother so meticulously sewed up in Haifa.

As we got dressed and exited the search cubicles, a big pile of dollar bills was conspicuously stacked up on the supervising officer's desk. Lutek, too, just went through the search and as he was about to leave the terminal he leaned over to me and whispered, "I got the same stuff, but couldn't you guys have used large bills?"

Two soldiers escorted us outside the terminal and shoved us into a Russian looking Jeep, and drove us to Pawiak prison. We were strip searched again, our personal effects, street clothing belts and shoe-laces were taken from us we were each issued a spoon and a tin cup and escorted to separate cells.

I spent a fitful night on a wooden cot with a straw mattress. My cell mates tell me that we are all being held by the Special Commission, which deals with black market issues, and that the typical minimum sentence is 5 years at hard labor.

Pawiak prison in Warsaw.

Some giant crack I stepped on this time! But for saving £10.00 at the consulate in Tel-Aviv, we could have been comfortably ensconced at cousin Regina's in Munich, awaiting our immigration visa for the USA.

118

I don't know what tomorrow will bring, but I will write you again as soon as I can.

Your loving future Papa

March 1st 1948

Dear Oscar and Emma,

It is now about two weeks since we got out of that terrible prison in Warsaw and I am writing to you from Szczecin, which is at the estuary of the Odra River on the Baltic Sea.

I spent a week in in that horrible place, patiently awaiting my fate. On the eighth day the cell door opened and a Polish prison guard took me to the guard room where I saw Oskar for the first time since we were locked up. They returned all our clothing and personal effects including a voucher for all the money which was confiscated at the airport, with instructions to retrieve the $300 at the State Bank and a stern warning not to engage in currency manipulation or black market. No doubt, all the serial numbers of the banknotes were duly recorded.

Although up to this point I took the lead and initiative in all matters concerning our destinations, travel etc. I became completely resigned and helpless in that prison. This time, Oskar, the scholar, rose to the occasion and wrote a long letter to the prosecutor handling our case, explaining that we were returning to Poland after a terrible war, and that we are most eager to continue our studies and become contributing citizens. The money, he explained came from our parent's savings and was meant to tide us over while we get settled in Poland, and was by no means meant for speculation or black market. We kept it concealed for fear of robbery. With that the prosecutor, accepted our plea and dismissed the case against us.

We picked up the money at the bank exchanged a few $ at the official rate which was a pittance in comparison to what it would bring on the black market.

Warsaw looked bleak in the winter and after our experience there, we decided to go to Sosnowiec, our home town, hoping to find some people we knew, and to plan our next move. Once we got there, we went to a local café, where we ran into Mr. Manela, a local optician who used to fill prescriptions for Father's patients. He told us that Dr. Rzendowski, a colleague of Father's, who treated me for pleurisy during the war and once saved us from deportation, was in Sosnowiec.

Upon arriving at his apartment, we met with the same astonishment as we did in Prague.

"You mean to say that you left Palestine to come back to Communist Poland, even as all the survivors are trying to go there? As a matter of fact, my wife and I are planning to do so, and my son Jurek just left for Mexico to study."

Despite his attitude he was very hospitable and put us up for a couple of days.

It occurred to me that although we missed our chance at the Chech-German border, Poland, too, had a border with Germany. After consulting the map we decided to go to Szczecin which was a German city before the war. At the end of the war, the Polish borders shifted westward, The Soviets grabbing the eastern Polish part of

Belarus, and the Poles annexing the eastern part of Germany up to the Odra River.

Before leaving for Szczecin I decided to check on the "treasure" I buried with my grandfather at the beginning of the war. I first went to grandfather's apartment building courtyard, only to discover that all the wooden lockers were gone and the entire courtyard was freshly paved over. Discouraged and disappointed I did not even go near the store. We caught the train for Szczecin on the same day.

Although it was three years after the end of the war, Szczecin still looked devastated. Bombed out hulks of buildings, empty lots filled with rubble, facades pock-marked by shrapnel, a bleak sight, indeed.

The bulletin board at the train station was filled with offers of rooms for rent. Picking one at random we walked a few blocks to a third floor apartment of Mr. and Mrs. Stabach, who showed us to a bright, sunny room with two beds, a dresser, wardrobe, two chairs and a small table, where I am sitting now, as I write to you. We ac- cepted it immediately and paid a modest sum for the first month's rent.

For the last few days we have been looking for employ- ment. The prospects are very good, as this city can use all the help it can get.

Before I end this letter I have to tell you about our land-lords. Mr. Stabach is a real character. He is a lanky tall redhead with permanent red stubble and an unkempt red moustache. He works in the city sewers and wears a filthy, stained one-piece military overall with a matching Polish four-cornered military cap. He never changes his attire. He begins each morning with a hearty breakfast consisting of a giant slice of bread and a dozen scrambled eggs. The reek of the sewer hangs like a pall on his overalls, and is only mitigated at the end of his work day by the smell of vodka which he apparently imbibes in throughout the day.

Despite his appearance the man is incredibly witty has a great sense of humor and never loses his temper, despite the constant hen-pecking of Mrs. Stabach. He took and instant liking to me and tries to corner me at every chance to share yet another tall tale. Mrs. Stabach is the complete opposite. She is very quiet, kind and soft spoken and meticulously clean. How she can coexist with that man is hard to comprehend.

Mr. Stabach. came back from work this afternoon and told me that S.U.M., the Szczecin Maritime Bureau is desperately looking for all kinds of help in connection with the reconstruction of the bombed out port.

So tomorrow we will go to S.U.M and fill out applications for a job. After Warsaw, maybe things will turn for the better.

I am closing for now and promise to write again soon. Your

loving future Papa.

July 31st 1948

Dear Oscar and Emma,

Sorry I didn't write to you sooner, but so many things happened since I got to Szczecin, that there was no chance to concentrate on bringing you up to date.

This morning after two arduous weeks of physical exertion I flunked the medical examination for acceptance to the Polish Merchant Marine Academy. I am writing to you from the waiting room of the Gdynia RR station. Since my train for Szczecin is not due for another three hours, I have ample time to bring you up to date.

No sooner that we arrived at the S.U.M. last March, we were both offered employment. Oskar got a clerical position in the administration. Thanks to my drafting course at the technical school in Tzfat, I was placed in the engineering department where I would do some clerical work and drafting.

My immediate superior and mentor is Mr. Zbigniew Koscinski on the S.U.M. staff. He is very formal and addresses me as Mr. Horowitz. I am not used to this at age

126

eighteen and though I ask him to address me by my first name, the best he can do is to call me Mr. Rudek.

Mr. Koscinski is about thirty years old. He chain smokes smelly cheap cigarettes through a slim cigarette holder, and seldom parts with his naval captain's hat adorned with a gold embroidered griffon insignia.

The head of engineering is engineer Tadeusz Romalski. He usually keeps himself ensconced in his private office. An impressive gentleman of about forty with a shock of light blond hair, blue eyes, an aquiline nose casting a shadow over his immaculate trim mustache, always wearing tweed plus-four suits with argyle socks and tie to match and sporting freshly pressed starched shirt every morning. He is a picture of true Polish nobility, who could easily make it on the big screen. It makes me wonder where he gets all of that in post war Communist Poland.

Although my daily work was quite easy and routine, three events took place within the first few weeks which made things a lot more challenging and interesting.

Koscinski got a free-lance assignment to prepare construction drawings of a giant crane grab bucket, by disassembling and measuring parts of the demolished buckets in the harbor. He asked me whether I would be willing to prepare the detailed final drawings if he did the disassembly, measuring and rough sketches of each

127

part. The work was to be done on our own time, after regular work day and on weekends. The only drawback was that we were not to get paid until the job was completed and approved. I, of course, accepted immediately.

The next event took me completely by surprise. Engineer Romalski approached me one afternoon and asked me if it was true that I knew English. I told him I was fluent. Would I be willing to give him and his wife private lessons at their home for a fee. Looked like more private enterprise in Stalinist Poland. Again, I accepted unhesitatingly.

And finally the third event which would give me more pleasure and enjoyment than anything I experienced in Poland hitherto.

One afternoon when Koscinski and I were roaming the harbor looking for crane bucket parts, he asked me if I have ever been on a sailboat. I said no, as the only time I had been on the water in my life was on a transport ship from Marseille to Haifa. It turns out that the reason for his naval cap with the Griffon insignia was his position as vice-commodore of the local Yacht Club Gryf which kept him busy sailing every weekend from spring to fall. Before he managed to utter an invitation I asked him how soon we could go. He promised that as soon as the weather got warmer, about mid-May he would take me out sailing.

When the Polish border shifted westward at the end of

the war and the Germans fled, they did not leave just the ruins. Among other things they left behind six Shore-Cruiser (Schärenkreuzer) yachts in mint condition. These boats became the nucleus of Koscinski's yacht club.

A Schärenkreuzer similar to the ones in the Club Gryf.

The following Saturday I went to the Romalski house to give my first English lesson. The house is in a beautiful residential neighborhood of expensive single family homes. It is virtually untouched by the war. The interior is filled with ornate, expensive furniture, lots of crystal and paintings, no doubt as the German owners must have left it in their hasty strategic withdrawal.

Mrs. Basia Romalski is a beautiful brunette, perfectly coiffed, dressed in what appears like the latest Parisian fashions. Together they look like they stepped out of the pages of a movie magazine. The whole image is completely out of character with the current conditions in Poland. I am thinking: he must be either vital to the reconstruction effort, or else be a big-shot in the Communist

Party. As I settle to teaching them basic expressions and phrases using a Polish-English textbook, it is obvious that Mr. R. is catching on quickly, readily absorbing everything I offer, except for his pronunciation. Every word containing a soft or hard "th" sound, he pronounces as a resonant "zzzz". Basia, in turn, is totally inept. She seems unaware of my attempts at instruction, keeping her eyes on her husband and trying to repeat everything he says. Soon the room sounds like a busy beehive. What the heck, I am thinking, they are both nice to look at, and I am getting paid for it.

The second weekend in May Mr. Koscinski asked me to meet him at the Gryf dock on the Odra river for my first

sail. The sleek sailboat hull about ten meters long, all

mahogany, was freshly varnished, revealing perfectly butted, curved planking from stem to stern. The deck planking is teak. The slender mast reaches skyward, with a gentle curve toward the stern at the top.

The sails, made of Egyptian cotton canvas, are very heavy. I learn quickly how to hoist and lower the sails, how to tack and steer the boat, how to kedge it off the shoals, which we get stuck on quite frequently. The sailboat has no auxiliary power, so the only way to propel it when becalmed, is single-oar sculling. By now I am very proficient at it.

It is about 18 miles up the Oder to the open waters of the Szczecin Lagoon, and the sail can be very challenging. Besides the constant tacking in the narrow river channel one must be constantly aware of the ocean-going ships and river barges exercising their right-of-way over our small vessel.

Although sailing has become a great joy for me, the thought of getting out of Poland never leaves my mind. I even fantasize about stealing one of the little yachts and sailing off to Sweden.

Earlier this summer, while roaming the harbor in connection with my crane bucket assignment, I became acquainted with a second officer on a Polish cargo vessel. He had Jewish parents who perished in Auschwitz, and in many respects his background is similar to mine. He expressed his complete disgust toward the Communist Regime in Poland and offered that the only reason he was still around is because he was making good money sailing all over the world and could jump ship in the West if things got too hot.

When I confided in him that I was desperately looking for a way out, he suggested that I follow his example, by applying to the Polish Merchant Marine Academy, getting a degree and a deck officer's commission and then skipping out at will while abroad.. Moreover, he indicated, I wouldn't have to wait for a degree, as the cadets spent every summer

The Polish training square-rigged ship "Dar Pomorza"

cruising to foreign ports in the west, on the four-masted square-rigger "Dar Pomorza". With that he wrote down all the information pertaining to the application for admission.

I sent out my application in early July and within a week I received a reply accepting me for a two week camp tryouts at the Academy in Gdynia. The next morning I went to my boss, Eng. Romalski to request a vacation or a leave of absence. Since Romalski had just left on vacation, I asked Koscinski to offer my apologies to the boss upon his return, explaining my dilemma.

The first week of camp was mainly physical. We marched ran, jumped climbed, did calisthenics, short order drill, underwent swimming tests etc. It was intend- ed primarily to weed out the weaklings . I managed to get through it without too much difficulty.

The second week was much more arduous. It was conducted mainly on the water and frequently out in the open sea. My single-oar sculling experience came in handy. Except that this time instead of a sleek yacht, I had to propel a monstrous twenty foot lifeboat with a single heavy ten foot oar from the stern. I did better than most. We went out daily, twelve to a life boat into the open Baltic and rowed for hours in calm water in swells, in waves, against breaking surf. We learned to scull and feather the oars and retrieve shipmates tossed overboard into the waves. Yesterday was the last day. At dinner the head instructor called out the names of all the candidates who made it. I breathed a sigh of relief when my name was called. The instructor congratulated us saying that the only thing left is the formality of final medical exam scheduled for the following day.

This morning, after breakfast, we were marched to the parade ground and told to strip to our waists and line up in a row facing the instructor. The doctor, arrived (he had a stethoscope hanging around his neck) and proceeded with the examination. He stepped up to each candidate, with the instructor close behind him, placed the stetho-scope on the candidate's chest listened to one or two heartbeats and uttered a single word, "Pass". This went on routinely until he came in front of me. He barely touched me with the stethoscope when he uttered, "Heart defect". The instructor asked me to step out of the line expressed his regrets and told me to go to the office and get my ticket for the return to Szczcin.

I hear the sound of a distant whistle, and my train is due any moment now. I see a mailbox on the platform, so I'll post this before boarding my train. Tomorrow is Sunday so I will have a day to relax before going back to work.

Hugs and kisses to both of you ,

From your loving future Papa

August 1st 1948

Dear Oscar and Emma,

Although I just wrote to you yesterday, I feel I must share

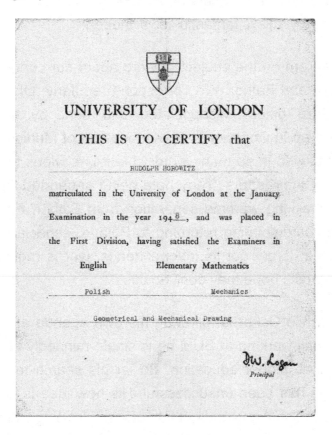

UNIVERSITY OF LONDON

THIS IS TO CERTIFY that

RUDOLPH HOROWITZ

matriculated in the University of London at the January Examination in the year 194 8 , and was placed in the First Division, having satisfied the Examiners in

English   Elementary Mathematics

Polish   Mechanics

Geometrical and Mechanical Drawing

JW. Logan
Principal

my latest good news with you at once. On my return to Szczecin last night I found a letter from Mother and Father from Haifa addressed to me alone. This was unusual because the letters we usually get from them are addressed to both Oskar and me. On opening it I discovered to my immense surprise and joy that I passed the London University Matriculation in the First division. The certificate was enclosed. I suppose the First Division must be better than the Second Division. Considering the disappointment of having washed out of the Academy and my lingering doubts about the exams I took in Haifa in January, this is fantastic news, indeed.

While I am on the subject, a word about our contact with Mother and Father. We correspond regularly. Of course, they are bitterly disappointed and unhappy that we wound up in Communist Poland instead of Munich. They don't say so in so many words, but it is obvious from the tone of their letters. They hate being separated from us after the long wartime separation from Father. Father is even contemplating returning to Poland, especially since now that Israel got its independence, war is raging with the Arabs. I hope they don't do this.

Meanwhile Oskar is following his own agenda and interests. Still working at SUM he is single-mindedly pursuing one goal: higher education. So far his search for scholarships has been unsuccessful. His new idea is to enlist in the Polish Army and get into officers' training which is a path to a university degree. I think the notion is crazy and I tell him so. But that is Oskar. He would be happy on the moon if he could study and bury himself in books.

Never mind that it would seal his fate forever in Communist Poland.

I will close for now, with love and hugs,

Your future Papa.

August 16th 1948

Dear Oscar and Emma,

The latest news is that I have a new job since I last wrote.

The Monday after I returned from the Maritime Camp in Gdynia, I was summoned to Engineer Romalski's office who told me that I was fired effective immediately. The reason was gross negligence of my duties, leaving for two weeks without permission and a generally poor attitude toward my work. No amount of pleas and explanations did any good. I was to pack all my personal stuff, I'd be paid for the days I was at camp and my brief ca- reer at S.U.M. was over. This also ended my budding teaching career.

This did not affect Oskar. He continues at whatever he was doing on the second floor of the building.

I was not too worried about my immediate prospects, as jobs of all kinds are plentiful in Szczecin. Mindful of my ultimate goal to get out of Poland and go to the US, I thought the best course would be to find employment in or near the harbor.

Although Koscinski and I had free access to most of the harbor during our crane bucket days, there were sections of the port which were fenced off and guarded by the Polish Military Border Police. These sections contained the piers where foreign cargo ships arrived to discharge their cargo and take on Polish coal. The only civilians allowed in this restricted area were representatives of shipping brokers who dealt with the formalities of cargo clearance, bills of lading and all matters of import and export.

On one occasion last spring I struck up a conversation with one of these brokers, and asked him if it was difficult to get such a job. He said, it was easy, if you knew at least one foreign language.

Two days after my firing I presented myself at the Szudzinski Shipping Broker Agency. It is located on the second floor of a large apartment building. The doorbell was answered by a friendly young man with a pleasant smile and penetrating blue eyes. After I introduced myself and stated my purpose, he said his name was August Paszkudzki, but I should feel free to call him Gucio (*Goo-tchoh*). When he found out that I was fluent in English, he enthusiastically countered, "You're just who we've been looking for", rushing out to get his bosses, Mr. Szudzinski and Ms. Malgorzata. After a brief chat – hardly an interview -- I was told to come in and start training the following day.

That was just a couple of hours ago when I came home to write this letter.

Will keep you up to date as things develop.

Your devoted future Papa

November 28ᵗʰ 1948

Dear Oscar and Emma,

A lot of interesting things happened since my last letter, but the most disturbing occurred last week, when Oskar and I were summoned to appear at the local U.B. Office. This is the notorious Polish version of GPU, the Soviet secret police famous for sending dissenters or critics of the regime to Siberia. We were advised that the purpose of our summons was interrogation. Arriving at the appointed time, we were kept waiting for many hours in the reception area with no hint of what it was all about. Finally, toward the end of the day, our names were called out and the man behind the counter told us that we could go home. The uncertainty of the situation compounded our anxiety and I began to search my mind as to what incident could have brought this on.

This brings me back to where I left off at my last writing. Gucio Paszkudzki and I became fast friends. Since at 26, he is much older than I, I treat him with respect and admiration, and he, in turn, being an only son looks upon me as his younger brother. We spend many hours together, telling and retelling the experiences of our young lives over liberal portions of cheap polish vodka.

Gucio, who is a gentile, is married to Renata, an attractive young Jewish woman, whom he saved along with her entire family from the Nazis during the Holocaust, by hiding them in the cellar of his parents' house. Toward the end of the war he joined the Polish underground in the forests and fought the Nazis as they were retreating from the advancing Red Army. For this the Soviets with their U.B. lackeys arrested him, tortured him knocked a few of his teeth out and imprisoned him for months. Apparently, you could fight the Nazis only on the Soviets' behalf. Doing so as part of the Free Polish Army could buy you a trip to the salt mines.

Gucio showed me the ropes and I quickly found that the work was quite easy and routine. It involved filling out bills-of-lading and other documents connected mainly with the export of Polish coal to Sweden. Occasionally the ships bring Swedish iron ore to Poland, but they generally arrive empty to take on the coal. Initially, I tag along with Gucio observing and absorbing it all and within a couple of weeks I am on my own.

While I am on the subject of my new job I must not forget to mention what Gucio told me in confidence over a couple of drinks, recently. Apparently one reason I was hired so readily was that Szudzinski and his partner, Ms.

Malgorzata suspected, I was a U.B., secret police plant placed in their office to spy on them. Not wanting to raise any suspicions they felt it was better to hire me and to have me on their own turf.

My official pass issued by the military border authorities and the Captain of the Port gives me unrestricted access to all parts of the harbor and allows me to board the for-

In my new custom tailored suit

eign vessels docked there. This must be an important and enviable position as all the local officials treat me with deference, address me as "Mr. Broker", tipping their hats as I walk by; the border guards salute when they see me, and I walk around like a peacock in my brown herringbone topcoat and brown fedora, clutching a thick leather briefcase, the symbol of my authority. On the plus side I am earning more money than I did at SUM. In fact enough to afford a tailor made double-breasted suit.

Most of the Swedish captains are very young. They speak German and English in addition to their native

Swedish. They welcome the chance to speak English and on occasion like to be entertained by going out to some of the local nightclubs. Acting as their companion and translator is one of my more enjoyable duties.

The task of clearing the loaded vessel for departure involves an officer and a soldier from the border service, a customs inspector, a harbor representative and me, representing the shipping broker. It is my responsibility to arrange for all these individuals to meet at a scheduled time on board the ship in the captain's stateroom/office. Stacks of documents are filled out in triplicate, quadruplicate, signed, countersigned, stamped all over (they love stamps, here) and finally distributed to all present. As this goes on the border guard checks the crew quarters for contraband. Finally as we are finished, we bid the captain farewell and go ashore. The pilot boards the ship to guide it into the open sea as it sails for Sweden.

I go through this several times a week and it has become so routine, I can do it with my eyes shut. On one such recent occasion, as we were all concentrating on the paperwork, the border guard burst into the stateroom, triumphantly holding up a bottle of vodka in each hand, followed by a Swedish crewman with a sheepish expression on his face. The Polish officer took down the seaman's name, confiscated the liquor and explained to him, with myself translating, that he broke the law and that he was immune from arrest as long as he is aboard ship which is Swedish soil, but is subject to arrest and prosecution as soon as he steps ashore. It was like a scene from a comic opera; all over a couple of bottles of booze, which the Swede, would no doubt have consumed by the time they reach Sweden. As an aside, and purely in jest, I quietly asked the soldier if he expected a promotion for his unique find. When we got ashore the officer to whom the soldier reported what I had said, took me aside and declared sternly that I had "insulted the dignity of the Polish uniform", a crime which, yes, is punishable by heavy fines and a prison sentence. I, of course, apologized immediately, explaining that I was joking and would never do it again. The officer left without further comment leaving me anxious as to whether he would act on his threat. And now I am wondering if my summons to U.B. was in connection with this incident.

Early this month, Mrs. Stabach rented a vacant room in the apartment to two girls who came straight from the farm, looking for work in the big city. A couple of days later I noticed that half the dollar bills, which we kept "hidden" among our clothes in the dresser drawer were gone. I told Mrs. Stabach that I suspected her two new tenants of the theft and that I was on my way to report it to the police. When I came back from the police station Mrs. Stabach told me that she threw out the two "tramps", but not before they replaced every bill they took in the drawer where they found them. I rushed back to the police station explaining that I made a mistake, that the money was misplaced and that I needlessly accused the girls of theft. So now I wonder, perhaps this was a cause of my summons.

I am getting increasingly anxious and cannot help thinking that unless I get out of Poland soon; I'll wind up in prison

I am closing for now, but will write again, soon.

Your loving future Papa.

January 19th, 1949

Dear Oscar and Emma,

The holiday season came and went. There is a lot of ice on the river and the ship traffic is a lot lighter than last November. Szczecin is dreary and depressing. The thought of somehow getting out of Poland never leaves me. From time to time I hear stories of some brave individual sneaking aboard ship, hiding and stowing away to Sweden. Few of them make it. The ones who don't are arrested and thrown into prison. The word is that in the Gdynia harbor, the border patrol inspects the departing vessels accompanied by bloodhounds.

A few days before the New Year, Gucio told me, while I was out of the office on an assignment, a plain-clothesman from the U.B. came by and spent nearly an hour with Szudzinski asking questions about me. Later on, Mr. S told me about his conversation with the U.B. man, but he did not have a clue as to what it was all about. There were some hints about loyalty, and whether I could be trusted with a harbor pass, but nothing specific.

Now I know I must get out without delay. I also know that I cannot go without Oskar. Mother and Father would never forgive me. Thankfully, last November Oskar's application to join the Polish Army Officers Corps was rejected, so that crazy idea is now history.

Two weeks ago the manager and single employee of our branch office in Kołobrzeg suddenly quit and left the office empty with no one to take care of the business. Kołobrzeg, is a small harbor along the Baltic coast about half way between Szczecin and Gdynia, and like those two harbors is primarily engaged in exporting coal to Sweden.

Szudzinski, and his partner/girlfriend Malgorzata are unwilling to forfeit their share of the business to the only small competing firm, there. They are looking for a quick solution. Unfortunately, I appear to be the answer to their problem, and they tell me that I will have to move to Kołobrzeg, to head up that office. I thank him for his confidence and trust in me but indicate my reluctance to leave my place in Szczecin where all my friends are and where I am quite happy, thank you. Then I suggested that instead of reducing the Szczecin office staff, why not hire Oskar, my brother for the branch office. He speaks English and some German and I could teach him all I know about our business in two weeks. Szudzinski and Malgorzata agree that this is an excellent idea and Oskar is promptly hired.

Oskar started two days ago. By now he has his harbor pass, and today was our first joint appearance on a small Swedish freighter with me doing all the necessary paperwork and Oskar observing as the intern.

The funny thing about us working together is that a lot of the harbor staff familiar with my frequent visits there are doing double takes when they see those two identical brown topcoats and brown fedoras.

I am very anxious and fearful. At the same time I am hopeful that luck will turn my way and I'll skip over the giant crack looming in the distance.

Until the next letter,

Yours very hopefully, future Papa

February 9th, 1949

My dear Oscar and Emma,

It is exactly a year and a day since I wrote to you from that awful Pawiak prison in Warsaw. Here I am writing from jail, again. We were "arrested" and brought here yesterday, but I am jumping ahead; so let me pick up where I left off.

By the beginning of February, Szudzinski was anxious to send Oskar to Kołobrzeg. Although he was ready to take on the assignment, I stalled, telling the boss that there were still some things he was unfamiliar with and it would take another week to ten days to get Oskar up to speed. I knew that the only chance we had to get out of Poland was together, from Szczecin. Szudzinski reluctantly acceded to an additional week of training.

The typical freighters on the coal run between Poland and Sweden are not very large; they resembled ocean going barges with the engine room and the entire superstructure, bridge, officers' quarters, etc. located in the stern of the vessel. All the cargo holds are located forward, with the crew quarters up in the forepeak.

The s/s Brittmarie which docked on February 1st, is at least twice the size of the aforementioned vessels, has a profile of a traditional ocean going cargo ship with the engine room and entire superstructure, funnel, etc. located amidships, and its giant cargo holds, fore and aft. I was assigned the task of clearing it in on arrival and subsequent departure. Since the ship came in empty, the formalities connected with its arrival were over quickly and the local bureaucrats went ashore. Captain Carlsson, whom I just met for the first time asked me to stay for a while and invited me to share a drink. He spoke excellent English and told me that he seldom meets Polish brokers who speak the language, and that he welcomed the chance to relax and chat. We spent a very pleasant half hour together.

As I was about to leave, I somehow got the courage to share with him my fears that the secret police was after me and I faced arrest and imprisonment if I didn't get out of Poland soon. Stowing away on the Brittmarie would save me from a life of misery. The Captain got up from his chair and told me sternly that although I sounded sincere he had no way of knowing if I myself was not a member of the secret police acting as a provocateur and trying to get him in trouble with the authorities. He knew of at least one such case, which took place in Gdynia. He was not about to fall into a trap, as he was totally apolitical, especially in Poland.

151

With that he walked over to his desk, removed a large folded document from the drawer and spread it on top of the desk. We are both looking at detailed plans and cross sections of his ship. Tracing his finger over various portions of the drawings, he murmurs half to himself, pointing out which are the good hiding places on the Brittmarie. Elated, I spontaneously throw my arms around him in a big hug thanking him for trusting me despite his misgivings. I go ashore full of anxiety and hope.

Based on the ship's tonnage I calculate that it will take about 2 ½ days to load it, and if they finish loading on Thursday the 3rd, it should sail the following morning. Obviously, I cannot clear the ship out and hide and stow away on it at the same time. So Thursday morning I stayed home from work, while Oskar went to work reporting that I came down with the flu and was running a fever. That evening we packed a few personal effects some papers and the dollars in our briefcases and headed for the harbor. The Brittmarie was brightly illuminated with floodlights and the cranes were busy loading coal into her holds. Judging by how high she was floating I knew that she had a lot more cargo to take on and would not sail the next day. As I turned to go home, I had the bad luck to bump straight into Szudzinski. He was there to see the progress of loading, as he had to fill in for my bedridden self the next day at the ship's sailing. Dumbfounded and at a loss for words I quickly concocted a story about picking up some fabric that one of the captains on another ship was bringing from Sweden for his girlfriend, Malgorzata. Yes, I still felt sick and feverish, and got up from my sickbed to do this for her, and no, I doubt if I'll be able to get to work tomorrow. Visibly angry, Szudzinski told me to get the hell out of there, go home, and that he would deal with me appropriately when I get back to the office.

The following day we waited till past 9 pm., when the harbor activities and traffic settle down, before we ventured out. In the harbor we moved furtively, sticking to the shadows, intent upon avoiding any unexpected encounters. Near the ship we passed a border guard whom I knew quite well. I commiserated with him about being out in such cold weather – it was well below freezing at the time. He thanked me for my concern and offered that his shift was almost over and he would be heading for a warm bed. I made a mental note that his relief would not be aware of us boarding the ship.

By now the Brittmarie was settled way down in the water, but the loading was still continuing. Two cranes, one fore and one aft kept swinging back and forth dumping coal into her gaping holds. The whole area was brightly illuminated with floodlights, both on shore and aboard ship. We went straight to the Captain's cabin. He was very upset because it took a day longer to take on the cargo than he expected and the delay was costing his company money. He, accordingly, scheduled an early 6 am departure.

Despite his annoyance, Captain Carlsson was expecting us and told me that he had tied a rope at the top of one of the giant ventilators which forces air into the interior of the ship as it moves forward. We were to climb down the rope, which he would then remove after us.

When we got to the ventilator, we saw that it led straight down into a corner of the cargo hold still being loaded. Several stevedores were down below working with shovels and directing the crane bucket where to dump its load. There was no way we could get down that rope unnoticed.

Back in the Captain's cabin I was getting desperate. He calmed me down, suggesting another, even better hiding place, the coal-bunker.

The bunker contains coal, which is not part of the cargo, but is used to fuel the steam engine running the ship. It is located amidships on either side of the engine room and is loaded through hatches on the upper deck, on either side of the bridge. He handed me a flashlight and suggested that we head for the hatch on the waterside of the ship, which would be in the dark. Although the hold was almost completely filled with coal there were voids around the edges of the hatch through which we climbed in easily.

There was adequate room to move around as we looked for a good hiding place. The coal fell through the hatch, tumbling down along a 45-degree slope, creating a small triangular tunnel between the bulwarks (the outside wall of the ship) and the deck above. Crawling into this space we settled into a fetal position with our feet against the bulwarks and our knees up against our chins. In this contorted position, we managed to fill the triangular space on either side of us with loose coal, so that from the outside it appeared as if the space were filled in

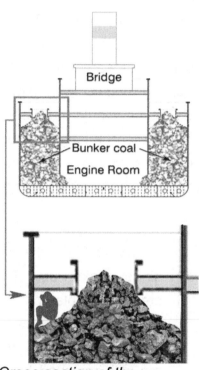

Cross section of the Brittmarie showing our hiding place in the coal bunker

solid with coal.

It was now past midnight. We were freezing. Although we wore most of the clothes we owned, it didn't make up for the below zero weather and the ice on the river separated from our frozen feet by ¼ " of cold steel. Moreover, there was no way to move to improve circulation in this confined space. Setting all that aside I concentrated on the events outside. By 1:30 am the cranes were silenced. No more noise of tumbling coal. It was followed by the sound of the giant hatch covers being lowered and secured in place. Silence and waiting followed. At 5 am I hear sound of footsteps above. I can picture Szudzinski mad as hell for taking my place at this early hour. I also imagine the border patrol coming aboard with bloodhounds, for the first time in Szczecin. Would that be my undoing? I shake with cold and fear for the longest hour I spent in Poland since landing in that prison a year ago. More footsteps and running on deck above us. Then silence.

Route of the Brittmarie

Finally at 6 am the engines wake up. The steady rumble of the engines is a sweet sound indeed and fills me with renewed hope. The Polish pilot is now guiding the Brittmarie into the open Baltic. All the way up the Odra into The Szczecin Lagoon, through the canal at its north end and into the open sea. This takes about three hours. By now the heat from the engine room makes our hiding place more bearable. At noon I hear the engines straining into re-verse, then stop, and 15 minutes later we are underway again. I assume we are a couple of miles offshore and the pilot just climbed down a ladder into a launch, which will take him back to Szczecin. Though I am still in the coal-bunker, I know from experience that this is what is happening above, on deck.

Though I know we are free, I am still plagued by doubts. What if I miscalculated and the pilot is still on board? What if they discover my absence in Szczecin and a Polish patrol boat gives chase, stops the ship and arrests us? What if Captain Carlsson has a change of heart and upon seeing us turns the ship around and delivers us back to the Poles? I know this is all nonsense, but I de-cide it best if we spend another 3 hours in our hiding place before presenting ourselves to the captain.

At 3 pm we emerge on the windswept deck and head for the captain's cabin. He grabs his flashlight from me and tells me that nobody knows about us "including himself", and that we should report to the deck officer on the bridge. We climb the companionway to the bridge. The first officer is a short man about 5' tall, with an enormous white walrus mustache wearing a captains cap, a pea coat and knee high fur lined boots. Looking toward the bow he scans the horizon with his binoculars. As he piv-

157

ots around we come into his view. Dropping the glasses he lets loose with a string of oaths, only one of them familiar: "Jävla fan Polacker!" Goddam it, Polacks! He gets on his horn and calls the captain. The captain arrives on the bridge, feigns surprise, curses and yells in Swedish, then pausing pretends to look at me closely and in a mixture of Swedish and English, so his mate will understand, he says to me,

"Although you look like you just came out of a coal mine, you look familiar; aren't you working for the broker who cleared our ship in?" I replied that yes I am and that my brother and I are escaping Polish Communism. He countered this: I am complicating his life; he's a simple freighter captain he will have a lot of explaining and paperwork on our account, and asks us to follow him to his cabin.

Shutting the door behind him he pulls out a bottle of Aquavit from his desk pours three glasses and wishing us good luck, offers a toast to our future. Expressing my gratitude for what he had done for us, I hand him $150 from our emergency fund. He is reluctant to accept it until I reassure him this was from our emergency fund for Poland, and now that we are out of Poland the emergency is over. Besides we still had over $100 between us and that the money I offered him is just a token and will never truly repay for what he did for us.

The rest of the trip was uneventful. In order to allay any suspicions on the part of his crew that he was complicit in our escape, the captain made it known to all that since we were getting a free ride to Sweden, we would be required to do some work during the passage. Thus I was helping him with paperwork in connection with the payroll, and Oskar was assisting the steward in the galley.

Our destination is Norrtälje, a small port along the east coast of Sweden, north of Stockholm, and situated at the end of a long inlet 16 miles distant from the open Baltic. We picked up the pilot at the mouth of the inlet, who was accompanied by the ship owner's agent. When captain Carlsson told him of our situation he went back ashore and phoned ahead advising the authorities in Norrtälje of our impending arrival.

We docked some two hours later and were met by two officers in a police car. In contrast to our previous experience with the authorities they treated us with utmost courtesy and respect. We were placed in a cell with two comfortable beds – not wooden cots – and the door to the corridor was left unlocked. What a difference a jail makes! We just finished lunch, which, like all jail meals, is catered by the local hotel, delivered by a beautiful Swedish blonde. The wicker basket it came in is wrapped in white linen and is filled with Swedish delica- cies, most notably, pancakes with lingonberries.

We were going to be interviewed on the following day, for the purpose of ascertaining that we were not fugitive criminals. Since we were going to be questioned sepa- rately, we resolved to tell the facts without embellish- ments or distortions. This way our stories would jibe and would not raise any suspicions.

I had one lingering concern. Count Folke Beradotte, a Swedish diplomat who was mediating the conflict be- tween the Arabs and the Jews on behalf of the United Nations, was assassinated in Jerusalem a few months ago by Jewish terrorists. I worried that there would be some resentment and suspicion when they find out that we were in Palestine before we came to Poland. Fortu- nately, the interrogation, conducted by a bald headed plainclothesman, was straightforward and concluded with no hiccups.

This morning I met two Danish fellows who occupied the adjacent cell. They had the run of the place and came and went as they pleased. When I asked them what they were in for, they laughed and told me that they had no money and no place to stay, so the police let them bed down for a couple of nights.

I told the constable on duty that like the Danes we have not committed any crime, so could we go out for a walk or go to a movie. After consulting the sergeant they agreed to let us go. Our first stop was the Post Office, where we dispatched a four-letter telegram to Mother and Father: "Arrived safely in Sweden". We then went to see "Incendiary Blonde", a Technicolor movie with Betty Hutton.

Upon returning to the Norrtälje jail the chief constable informed us that prior to our release to the relocation center we must undergo a physical examination and that he arranged an appointment with the local physician for later that afternoon.

We took advantage of the visit to the doctor to complain of a pesky itch, which bothered both of us since shortly before leaving Poland. No sooner did we strip to our waists than he diagnosed it as Scabies, a highly contagious skin condition resulting from infestation by a microscopic mite, which bores under the skin. The doctor called for an ambulance and asked us not to touch anything in his office. The ambulance took us to the local hospital, where we were placed in an isolation room and instructed to remove all our clothes placing our outer wear in a plastic bin and underwear in a paper bag.

161

Just as we finished stripping, two beautiful, blonde, twenty-something nurses entered the room armed with hemostats, packs of gauze and a basin containing an orange liquid. There was no time for embarrassment as they immediately proceeded to paint our entire bodies with this strange solution. Fortunately the room was quite cold which kept us from demonstrating physically our appreciation of their ministrations combined with their good looks. We were issued fresh underwear as our old stuff was incinerated. The outer garments were left out-doors in sub-zero weather, which is supposed to wreak havoc with those pesky mites.

I promise to write you again, as soon as I know more about our immediate future. In the meantime we are breathing free air in Sweden. And by the way, I love the Swedes!

Love, hugs and

kisses, from your

future Papa

July 14th 1949

Dear Oscar and Emma,

48 hours after our interrogation at the jail in Norrtälje last February, while still in the hospital, we were granted asylum in Sweden. Upon release from the hospital we boarded a bus for a nearby relocation camp at Gottröra.

Sven, a tall blond Swede in his late twenties, who was in charge of the place, met us at the camp. He explained in fluent English that we would stay at the camp until we find employment as well as living accommodations. There were about two dozen other people in a situation similar to ours. Most of them came from Poland, and all were very secretive about how they got there. I could understand that, as no one wanted to endanger any friends or relatives left behind. Accordingly, Oskar, and I too, resolved to keep mum about our escape.

A day or two after our arrival, Sven commenting on our coal stained clothes, suggested that we could obtain a loan to purchase new clothing and pay it off weekly from our paychecks when we get jobs. We accepted the offer eagerly.

On the following day we took a bus to a nearby town armed with a purchase requisition issued by the Swedish government and went shopping. While there was no limit on the requisition we were prudent in our purchases knowing that we were obligated to pay off the loan. At long last I was about to discard that tired brown tweed topcoat and replace it with a handsome leather jacket. My other indulgence was a pair of shoes with crepe soles. A few shirts and changes of underwear completed my new wardrobe. As we left the store I realized that habits die hard, observing that Oskar bought the exact same leather jacket and pair of shoes as I did. Mother must be proud of us.

When we returned to Gottröra Sven informed us that he secured jobs for Oskar and me at a foundry close by. Delighted with our new wardrobe and a new job we left the camp without delay.

The foundry was about an hour bus ride from the camp. On arrival there we were escorted to our housing, a factory dormitory for temporary and transient workers. The next morning we reported for work. Our assignment was to load wheelbarrows with sand for molds from a pile outside the plant and transport it inside close to the furnaces where the casting molds were made. It was back breaking labor. The sheer physical exertion of shoveling the sand into the wheelbarrow, pushing it a couple hundred yards into the building and dumping the stuff, was compounded by repeated exposure to freezing cold outdoors and sweltering heat next to the furnaces.

We lasted only one day. The following morning without saying a word, we packed our stuff and took the bus back to Gottröra. Surprisingly, Sven was not at all angry, to the contrary he apologized and admitted that he had no idea the work would be that hard. I reminded him

about my trade school training and he promised to find something more suitable for me and for Oskar.

A few days later Sven announced that he secured very good technical jobs for both of us at the Scania Vabis truck and bus factory in Södertälje. We left on the following day promising to hold on to our jobs and not surprising him again by returning to the camp.

Södertälje is a medium size town located 20 miles west of Stockholm, the capital of Sweden. Scania Vabis is the principal employer in Södertälje and a great place to work in. It is bright and clean and it has a great cafeteria where lunches are delicious and inexpensive.

My job is easy, simple yet very frustrating. I am assigned to operate an automatic lathe, which turns out a mysterious steel engine part shaped like a truncated top hat. The cutting tool when engaged follows a template, which turns the part to the desired profile. I have to make several passes to cut it down to proper size, and the proper size has a tolerance of one thousandth of an inch. Since I am very impatient I reduce the number of passes by making thicker cuts thus overheating the parts. Using a micrometer I measure the completed parts which meet specifications. When the inspector, a young Swede in a gray smock comes around to check my work, 90% of my work is rejected, as the pieces are under size having shrunk after cooling down. My bosses are very patient and they haven't fired me yet. They just urge me to be more careful and patient. How can you not love the Swedes?

Every Saturday evening there are dances in the local park. There are two dance floors with live music, one devoted to modern dances and the other to the Schottische and other folk dances. There is a distinct difference between the crowds at each venue. The girls who are partial to the Foxtrot and Lindy are prettier and much more stylish in their dress. Though they all enjoy dancing and are eager dance partners, few if any speak English, so communication is a constant barrier.

I made some friends at one of the dances who do speak English. Kurt Blom has the same job I had in Poland and works for a shipping agent. He has a rowboat, which he equipped with a mast and sail and offered me a ride on his vessel along the Södertälje canal.

Tommy is from Finland and though very likable he constantly gets on the subject of drugs and how much money you can make that way. Frankly, I have no idea what he is talking about.

Tommy and I in leather   *Tommy and Oskar in leather*

I bought an old decrepit one-speed bicycle, which I use for commuting and getting around town. Two weeks ago I heard through the grapevine that Richard Dugot, the boy who taught me to ride a bicycle in summer camp in 1939, survived the war and is living with his mother in Stockholm. Though Stockholm is, for some strange reason, off limits to asylum beneficiaries like me, I thought it would be fitting to ride my bike to Stockholm and surprise Richard. The distance of some 20 miles in one direction might be tolerable on a decent bicycle, but riding that beast of mine was considerably harder than a day at the foundry.

Unfortunately, I missed Richard as he was attending college. I left a message with his mother and asked that he get in touch and come and visit me in Södertälje.

Kurt Blom rowing his "yacht".

Sailing with Kurt is a blast and a joke. Since the boat does not have a centerboard tacking against the wind in the canal means that we are sailing from one shore to the other while staying in the same place.

Conversely, when the wind is with us we'd zip down to the

lake, which boasts a nudist beach club. There we take advantage of the lack of a centerboard. After stripping to our waists, with the wind on the bow as we face the club, we tack back and forth in front of the club, staying in one place and admiring the view.

It is very late and I have to get up early for work tomorrow, so I'll say so long for now,

With love and hugs,

Your future Papa

October 31st 1949

Dear Oscar and Emma,

You'll never guess where I am, as I am writing this letter. So let me first bring you up to date.

Last August, about a month after I wrote to you last, Richard came to visit us in Södertälje. It was a happy re-union considering that up to now he was the only one of our prewar friends who survived. Richard escaped from the ghetto just before its final liquidation and went to work on a German farm passing himself off as a gentile. His mother father and sister were sent to Auschwitz. Of the three only his mother survived and was with him in Stockholm.

Richard has been in Sweden long enough to acquire a decent command of the language. He is attending college in Stockholm, studying electronic engineering and working for L. M. Erickson a large electronic concern.

We spent a very pleasant Saturday together, the highpoint of which was a lively game of Ping-Pong in the local park. Perhaps too lively and vigorous, as I smashed my right thumbnail against the edge of the Ping-Pong table.

By the time I went back to work on Monday the thumb was swollen to double its size and the fingernail turned black and blue. When I visited the nurse's office I shamelessly declared that I accidentally hurt my thumb the previous Friday through carelessness next to a spinning lathe component. When asked why I didn't report my injury immediately, I responded that it did not look too bad or hurt too much when it happened. I was sent to see a doctor who dressed the wound and informed me that I would lose the fingernail and would be unable to work until a new one grows in.

On the doctor's recommendation Scania Vabis put me on an indefinite sick leave with pay. As a result I feel very dirty and guilty for being so dishonest. But, oh, how I still love the Swedes.

Taking advantage of my forced vacation I got in touch with Captain Carlsson of the Brittmarie, who was delighted to hear from me and invited me out to dinner in Stockholm. He took me to a restaurant in Gamla Stan (Old City) located in a cave two floors below street level. We had an excellent meal of several courses with different wines and cordials to top it off. At the end he insisted on picking up the tab, confessing that he still felt guilty for accepting my money.

At the beginning of September I received a letter from Father advising us that our application for US immigrant visas was transferred from Tel-Aviv to the US consulate in Stockholm.

On September 15th we got a registered letter from the US consulate in Stockholm informing us that our Polish quota numbers were next in line and to visit the consulate for the purpose of completing all the formalities for immigration. We went to Stockholm immediately, after which the consulate arranged with the Swedish government to issue to us alien/stateless passports to which our immigration papers would be attached.

The MS Gripsholm in New York harbor

By the beginning of this month we had the passports in hand and we were booked for passage on the MS Gripsholm from Gothenburg to New York, departing on October 21st 1949.

On October 14 I went to the Scania Vabis front office to tell them about my impending departure and to quit my job. While there I asked what to do about the outstanding balance on the loan for the clothing I purchased on arrival in Sweden. They called Sven in Gottröra, and put

172

me on the phone with him. Sven congratulated me offered his best wishes for a happy life in the US, and told me to forget about the unpaid balance and to consider it a gift from the Swedish people. Boy, I do love the Swedes!

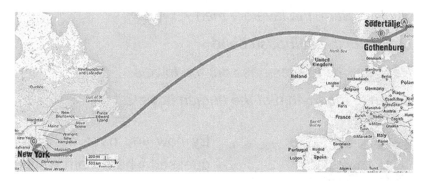

The ten-day voyage was uneventful except for the strange experience of trying to play Ping-Pong in a raging storm. The North Sea is very stormy at this time of the year and 20-foot waves are not at all uncommon. They account, however for a very strange trajectory of a Ping-Pong ball which aimed at the opposite side of the table misses its mark when the table and the ship lurch in the opposite direction.

My ping pong partner and frequent dinner companion is Mark, a college student from the Midwest returning from his summer vacation in Europe. Mark is obsessed with a dirty little ditty, which he sings all day long to a jazz beat. Willy-nilly I memorized it, so here with apologies is some of it:

173

Down in the cellar under the ground

Where all the poops go flopping around

Floppity flee, floppity floo

Listen to the rhythm of the outhouse blues

Stinking Sam, the lavatory man

Leader of the outhouse band

Pass out the tissues pass out the towels

Listen to the rhythm of the human bowels.

Aboard the MS Gripsholm en route to New York

By now you have no doubt guessed where I am writing this letter. In fact, about an hour ago the Gripsholm docked at pier 99, in the East River, at 59th Street in Manhattan. The American citizens have just started going ashore. The immigrants including Oskar and myself will be last as we have to be processed by the Immigration Service.

Before closing I must tell you about a strange day-dream I had as we were sailing past the Statue of Liberty. I closed my eyes and imagined the East River water parting between the New York and New Jersey shore,

174

revealing a giant crack in the riverbed stretching from shore to shore. Somehow, in my mind's eye the Gripsholm levitated, floating in the air above this gap and settling gently in the water on the other side. And so I skipped over the largest crack of them all.

Now I know I will be

Your future Papa

EPILOGUE

My first decade in America was a busy one. In the fall of 1950 I gained admission to the tuition free Cooper Union School of Art in New York, to study architecture.

In May 1951 I was drafted into the US Army and served for two years until the end of May 1953. After my discharge I completed my Architectural studies at the Cooper Union and the University of Michigan, graduating In 1958. In 1959 I went back to Europe for five months of study on the George G. Booth Traveling Fellowship from the University of Michigan.

Meanwhile, Mother and Father arrived in the US in 1953 and 1954, respectively. Father established a practice in Queens, New York after attaining his medical license.

Oscar went to MIT where he earned a Bachelor's, Master's and ultimately a PhD degree in Math and Physics.

During the next decade I worked for several architectural firms in New York, and passed the NY State Architectural license exam, 1n 1962 I married Betty and we became parents to Diana and David. In 1969, the year a man walked on the moon, we moved into our new house which

House in Pound Ridge

I designed and built in Pound Ridge, New York. We lived there for three decades.

In 1972 I established my own Architectural practice with offices in Pound Ridge and New York, concentrating on commercial and institutional projects. In the 1980's I developed GEOCAD, one of the earliest Architectural applications to AutoCAD as an adjunct to my Architectural practice.

On New Year's Day 2009, I began recording the most eventful decade of my life, 1939-1949. During that time I grew from childhood to adulthood, survived the Holocaust, traveled and lived in six different countries, and experienced Nazism, Communism and Zionism and on the last day of October 1949 my dream came true when I stepped ashore at Pier 99, on West 59th Street and the Hudson River, in Manhattan.

Made in the USA
Middletown, DE
15 April 2022

63982032R00106